OUT OF OUR MINDS

LEARNING TO BE CREATIVE

KEN ROBINSON

CAPSTONE

First published 2001 by
Capstone Publishing Limited (a Wiley Company)
The Atrium
Southern Gate
Chichester
West Sussex
PO19 8SQ
www.wileyeurope.com

CIP catalogue records for this book are available from the British Library and the US Library of Congress

ISBN-13 978-1-84112-125-3 (P/B)

Typeset in 10/14 Palatino by Sparks Computer Solutions Ltd, Oxford, UK
Printed and bound in Great Britain by TJ International Ltd, Padstow, Cornwall

20 19 18 17

In praise of **Out of Our Minds**

Competitive advantage does not come from the Internet. It comes from leveraging creativity. All corporate leaders should read this book.
Professor Richard Scase, author, *Britain in 2010*

If you would like to start to unlock the inherent creativity that exists in every human being (including you), then start … by reading this book!
Simon Woodroffe, founder Yo Sushi, and London Entrepreneur of the Year

Ken Robinson's is an original and creative mind. I can think of no better spokesperson on creativity. His views are as much directed to learning institutions as they are to industry. *Out of Our Minds* is a genuine challenge to complacency.
Ruth Spellman, Chief Executive, Investors in People, UK

I definitely want to meet Ken Robinson. I have a great affinity with the ideas he proposes. His writing is witty, sometimes caustic, and he supports his arguments with evidence and research. Robinson points us towards a future where young people must be enabled to unleash their creativity and deal with change through a different and better education system. As someone who gains a living from management development, this is all too evident to me. Robinson makes powerful arguments for change. I recommend that you read this book, take part in the debate and become part of the paradigm.
People Management

For a book called *Out of Our Minds*, Ken Robinson's illuminated assault on the current state of academic education is actually a very sane read. The current obsession is not only failing businesses but also our children. Robinson is right on the money.
Arts Professional

Out of Our Minds has a powerful agenda – how to solve the appalling lack of skills in a world demanding ever more brainpower. This is a thoughtful book that does not dodge such cruel paradoxes of our time as the fact that standards of living get higher while the quality of life declines: a truly mind-opening analysis of why we don't get the best out of people in a time of punishing change.
Director Magazine

By arguing for radical change in how we think about intelligence and the development of human resources, this book will stimulate and challenge those charged with investing resources in people. Importantly it should also stimulate them to recognize their own creative abilities and what inhibits their liberation.

Professional Manager

This is a deeply significant work in this area – I am really impressed with the historical perspectives and breadth of insights drawn from the arts, sciences, psychology and many other fields. It is an immensely powerful statement of the current educational situation and highlights very powerfully the need for transformed thinking from top to bottom.

Creative-Management

Out of Our Minds calls for radical changes in the way we think about intelligence, education and human resources, in order to meet the extraordinary challenges of living and working in the 21st century. This book will make compulsive reading for anyone who shares an interest in the future of creativity, education and training.

Center for Creative Communities

Sometimes a writer has an uncanny knack of sharply focusing something, which up until then you had not seen in all its simplicity and brilliance. This book does that but at the next moment it makes connections never before imagined … Even the most obstinately prosaic and safe thinkers will be tempted out of their box by Ken Robinson's ideas, theories and speculations. What's more, he writes as he speaks, in a way that, magnetically and compulsively, is simply irresistible.

Professor Tim Brighouse, Director of Education, Birmingham

There are certain books that manage to be authoritative, entertaining and thought-provoking and are also well written and richly exemplified. Few authors are able to fashion this attractive mixture. Alvin Toffler and Charles Handy can craft it. I add Ken Robinson's absorbing account of creativity to my personal list of gems. Creativity is one of those topics that excites some and enrages others. For Ken Robinson it is a universal talent that all people have, often without realizing it. Society in general and education in particular, can squash the imagination and rock self-confidence. I was sorry to reach the end of the text, as it had maintained its momentum throughout. The reading may finish, but the thinking goes on, just as you would expect from a book on this intriguing subject.

Professor Ted Wragg, London Times, Educational Supplement

CONTENTS

For Terry, who makes everything possible.

INTRODUCTION

I have a friend, Dave, who is an actor. He is a large actor, weighing about 20 stone or 280 pounds. He likes to drink beer and has a particular taste for a local beer called Abbot Ale. This is a powerful drink. You could run a small car – or a large actor – on Abbot Ale. Dave regularly drank 12 pints of it a day. Some years ago he developed back pain and went to his doctor, who referred him to a kidney specialist. The specialist examined him and said that he had potentially serious kidney problems. Dave asked what could be causing it. 'It could be a number of things', said the consultant. 'Do you drink?' David said that he did, socially, and mentioned the Abbot Ale. The specialist told him he would have to stop drinking or face the prospect of renal failure. Dave said he couldn't stop drinking, he was an actor. 'In that case', said the specialist, 'why don't you change to spirits?' Dave said he thought that spirits could cause cirrhosis of the liver. 'But you haven't come to see me about your liver,' said the specialist, 'I am concerned about your kidneys.'

This is an example of what in medicine is called the *septic focus*, the tendency to look at a problem in isolation from its context. A holistic doctor would recognise that the problem in Dave's kidneys was a result of his overall lifestyle; that it was the result of a broader problem. Solving that problem by causing another is no solution at all. The septic focus is evident in business and education every day.

There is a paradox. Throughout the world, companies and organisations are trying to compete in a world of economic and technological change that is moving faster than ever. As the axis shifts towards intellectual labour and services, they urgently need people who are creative, innovative and flexible. Too often they can't find them. Yet governments throughout the world are pouring unprecedented resources into the very process that's meant to develop natural talent and abilities – education. Political leaders emphasise their commitment to promoting creativity and innovation. They are pushing for higher and higher standards, and standards evidently are going up. Certainly children and students seem to be working harder than ever to gain academic qualifications. Why then does there seem to be a gap between the supply and demand for creative and innovative people. What's going wrong?

Businesses everywhere are spending large amounts of money trying to make people more creative. Like Dave's consultant, they are treating a problem without tackling its real causes. This, therefore, is not a conventional book on business creativity, offering tips for next week's course. It's about the root causes of the problem rather than a salve for the symptoms of it. It's only by seeing to the bottom of them that a realistic and genuinely effective strategy can be put together. This book offers answers to three questions that are now of vital importance for all companies, organisations and countries that have a serious strategic interest in creativity and innovation.

- *Why is it essential to promote creativity?* National governments, commercial companies and many other organisations are emphasising as never before the essential need to promote creativity and innovation. Why is it essential to do this? What is the price of failure?
- *Why is it necessary to develop creativity?* Why do so many adults think they're not creative (and not very intelligent) and that other people are? Most children are buzzing with ideas. What happens to them as they grow up? What's the real underlying problem?
- *What is involved in promoting creativity?* What is creativity, anyway? Is everyone creative or just a select few? Can creativity be developed and, if so, what can organisations do immediately to make the most of their creative resources? What are the benefits of success?

Creativity is often seen as a purely individual performance. It comes from people who just happen to be creative, or from departments whose role is to be creative. Most companies keep their 'creatives' in separate departments: they're the people who wear jeans and don't wear ties and come in late because they've been struggling with an idea. This book argues for a completely different approach, that:

- everyone has creative capacities, but they often do not know what they are;
- these capacities are the greatest resource available to an organisation; and that
- developing and exploiting creative capacities calls for a systemic strategy to generate a culture of innovation across the whole organisation including – but not only – the creative departments.

Organisations face three challenges in making the most of their creative potential and human resources. The first is to understand the real nature of creativity. This means countering the many misconceptions that are now blocking progress. The second is to implement a systemic strategy for developing individual creative capacities. There are techniques for doing this, which build on a number of common principles. Creativity can be developed, but it must be done sensitively and well. Most people do not know what their creative capacities are and are worried about the processes involved in finding out. Third, there must be a systemic strategy to facilitate and reward creative output. Occasional courses in creative thinking have limited value. Like rain-dancing, they underestimate the nature of the problems they are trying to solve.

One of the most fundamental problems is the very process that's meant to develop our natural abilities – education. Companies and organisations are trying to fix a downstream problem that originates in schools and universities. It would be naïve to think that education is simply a process of developing our natural abilities and rewarding achievements: that schools, colleges and universities simply sort out the intellectual sheep from the goats; that intelligent students do well and the less intelligent don't. Education doesn't just follow the natural grain of young people's abilities; it sorts them through two different filters. The first is *economic*: education categorises people on implicit assumptions about the labour market. The second filter is *intellectual*: education sorts people according to a particular view of intelligence. The problem we face now is that the economic assumptions are no longer true and the intellectual filter screens out some of the most important intellectual abilities that children possess. There are drastic consequences for the development of creative abilities. This was always a problem, but now it's getting critical.

There was a time when good academic qualifications guaranteed a job, but not any more. One reason is *academic inflation*. In the next 30 years, more people worldwide will be gaining academic qualifications than since the beginning of history. But as more people get them, their currency value is falling sharply. A university degree used to be an open sesame to a professional position. The minimum requirement for some jobs is now a Master's degree, even a PhD. What next? But there is a second problem. Many companies are facing a crisis in graduate recruitment. It's not that there aren't enough graduates to go around; there are more and more. But too many don't have what business urgently needs: they can't communicate well, they can't work in teams and they can't think creatively. But why should they? University degrees aren't designed to make people creative. They are designed to do other things and often do them well. But complaining that graduates aren't creative is like saying, 'I bought a bus and it sank'. This book suggests what all organisations, including educational ones, can do immediately to recover people's creative abilities. It argues for radical changes in corporate cultures to make the most of these resources.

Throughout this book, I develop three main arguments that apply with equal force to all companies and organisations with a serious interest in the sustained development of creativity, innovation and human capability.

- *We are caught up in a social and economic revolution.* This revolution is comparable to the Industrial Revolution of the 19th century and it has still hardly begun.
- *To survive it we need a new conception of human resources.* Current approaches to education and training are hampered by ideas of intelligence and creativity that have wasted untold talent and ability.
- *To develop these resources we need radically new strategies.* We won't survive the future simply by doing better what we have done in the past. Raising standards is no good if they're the wrong standards.

Facing the revolution

Business is caught in a revolution. The labour markets of the 21st century are changing beyond all recognition. This not a revolution in a figurative sense, but a real one comparable in scale and impact to the massive upheavals of the Industrial Revolution. This revolution is being driven like the last one by developments in technologies, and this one has hardly begun. Change is a constant factor in human history. What is distinctive now is the rate and scale of change. For most people, the Internet did not exist five years ago. It's now one of the most powerful forms of communication in history. Five years from now, it may be history itself as the next generation of microprocessors, based in nanotechnology, leads to the extreme miniaturisation of computers. Advances in neuroscience and genetics are converging with information sciences to create the possibility of microprocessors based in DNA, and of computer-enhanced intelligence. These technologies are transforming the nature of the work we do, how we work, who works and when and for how long. They are also generating many new social issues and cultural challenges. One of the most significant changes is the shift from manufacturing to the so-called knowledge-based industries.

New technologies are transforming the nature of work. They are massively reducing the numbers of people in industries and professions that were once labour-intensive. New forms of work rely increasingly on high levels of specialist knowledge and on creativity and innovation particularly in the uses of new technologies. These require wholly different capacities from those required by the industrial economy. Governments and businesses throughout the world recognise that education and training are the key to the future, and they emphasise the vital need to develop powers of creativity and innovation. First, it's essential to generate ideas for new products and services, and to maintain a competitive edge. Second, it's essential that education and training enable people to be flexible and adaptable so that businesses can respond to changing markets. Third, everyone will need to adjust to a world where, for most people, secure lifelong employment in single job is a thing of the past.

Someone leaving school in 1950 with good academic qualifications could expect a life of relatively stable employment, perhaps staying with the same company for a whole working life. This is no longer true. Few people seriously expect that young people leaving school in 2001 will be with the same company in 2041. Indeed, it seems unlikely that the company itself will still be there. Many people now expect to change not only jobs but occupations several times during their lives. The idea that schools can provide a direct route to secure employment in such a world merits a moment's thought. The price of failure is high. Throughout the developed world there is a growing problem of social exclusion particular among young people who are either unprepared or disinclined to join the search for employment. But the changes we all face are not only in work. These economic and technological revolutions involve equally profound changes in our ways of life.

Cultural communities are defined by their shared values and ways of living. In the last 50 years many of the old certainties have broken down; the nuclear family, patterns of religious involvement, gender roles and so on. These processes of cultural change are accelerating rather than slowing. Business expects the education system to give people the skills and qualities they need for this new world. The political response is to emphasise the need to raise standards. Of course we should. There's no point in lowering them. But standards of what? In these circumstances, political incantations about academic standards may seem a little feeble. They are.

You're more than you think

Education is a bad word to use socially. If you are at a party and tell someone you work in education they're likely to mumble about needing an early night. Many people expect to be as bored by the topic of education as they often were by the experience of it. But, if you ask them about their education, or about their children's, the opposite happens. They pin you to wall until you start looking at your watch. Many people have very deep anxieties about education. It's one of those issues like religion, politics and money that get among us. And it should. Education is vital to the success of our working lives, to our children's futures and to long-term national development. More than this, it stamps us with a deep impression of ourselves, and of everybody else, that's hard to remove. Success or failure in education can affect our image of ourselves for life. Those who don't show academic ability in school are often branded as less able. Some of the most brilliant and successful people in all walks of life that I know – or know of – failed in education. No matter how successful they have become, they carry within them a secret worry that they're not really as clever as they are making out. I know teachers, university professors, vice-chancellors, business people, musicians, writers, artists, architects and many others who failed at school. Many succeeded only after they'd recovered from their education. What about all of those who didn't? A major reason for this vast waste of ability in education is academicism: the preoccupation with developing certain sorts of academic ability to the exclusion of others, and its confusion with general intelligence. This preoccupation has led to an incalculable waste of human talent and resources. This is a price we can no longer afford.

As the technological revolution gathers pace, education and training are thought to be the answer to everything. They are, but we have to understand the question. Educating more people – and to a much higher standard – is vital. But we also have to educate them differently. The problem is that present expansion is based on a fundamental misconception: the confusion of academic ability with intelligence. For years academic ability has been conflated with intelligence, and this idea has been institutionalised into testing systems, examinations, selection procedures, teacher education and research. As a result, many highly intelligent people have passed through education feeling they aren't. Many academically able people have never discovered their other abilities. We have developed institutions and intellectual hierarchies on the assumption that there are really two types of people in the world, academic and non-academic: or as they are often called by common sense, the able and the less able.

The academic illusion

The problem is not promoting academic ability in itself, it is the obsessive preoccupation with it. Academic ability is a vital feature of human intelligence and in some respects is characteristic of it. One of the essential tasks of education is to develop academic ability to the best standards possible for everyone. But there's much more to intelligence than academic ability and much more to education than developing it. If there were no more to intelligence than this, most of human culture with its complex fabric of scientific, technological, artistic, economic and social enterprises would never have happened. There is an intriguing ambiguity in the idea of academic ability. On the one hand it is thought to be absolutely essential to individual success and to national survival. If academic standards are thought to be falling, the popular press beats its chest and politicians become resolute. On the other hand, 'academic' is used as a polite form of abuse. Professional academics are thought to live in ivory towers and have no practical understanding of the real world at all. An easy way to dismiss any argument is to say that it is merely academic.

How have we become so enthralled by academic ability and so contemptuous of it at the same time? The preoccupation with academic ability has specific historical roots in Western culture. These are partly philosophical and partly institutional. The roots of this obsession are deep in the Enlightenment, the massive expansion in European philosophy and practical science in the 16th and 17th centuries. This led to a view of knowledge and intelligence dominated by deductive reason and ideas of scientific evidence. These ideas have been reinforced since then by the styles of formal education, promoted especially through the public schools and universities. These methods of thought have had spectacular success in shaping our understanding of the world and in generating technological advances. But there has been a terrible price too.

The arts and sciences

One of the characteristics of this tradition is a division between the arts and the sciences. We live in a system where the sciences are associated with truth and objectivity, fact and hard reality, and the arts are thought of as being something to do with feeling, emotions and intuitions. The best that can be said is that they are a way of balancing education and giving children a fuller life of leisure and recreation outside work and employment. I remember having an argument on television about this with a prominent British politician. He said that the arts are really important because they help to educate people for leisure. The problem with this argument is that leisure is an idea that is relative to work. If you have less work, you may have more leisure. If you have no work, you're unemployed. That's quite a different feeling. At the time we had something like two million people in the UK who were unemployed. They were not organising themselves, to the best of my knowledge, as the new leisure classes.

The rationalist tradition has driven a wedge between intellect and emotion in human psychology; and between the arts and sciences in society at large. It has distorted the idea of creativity in education and unbalanced the development of millions of people. The result is that other equally important abilities are overlooked or marginalised. This neglect affects everyone. Children with strong academic abilities often fail to discover their other abilities. Those of lower academic ability may have other powerful abilities that lie dormant. They can all pass through the whole of their education never knowing what their real abilities are. They can become disaffected, resentful of their 'failure' and conclude that they are simply not very bright. Some of these educational failures go on to have great success in adult life. How many do not?

The second reason for the high levels of wasted ability is the view that there is a direct linear relationship between general education and subsequent employment. Because of this, schools are under pressure to prioritise those subjects that seem most relevant to the economy. It is argued that there is a national need to produce more scientists and technologists. Consequently, there is a high priority on science and technology in schools and provision for the arts and humanities is cut back to make way for them. This is the pattern in most developed countries. There are good reasons to doubt whether this policy is in the best interests of young people or of society in general or even whether it's the best way to produce good scientists and technologists. In any case, is a mistake to think of the relationship between education and the economy as a straightforward process of supply and demand, like producing biscuits or cars.

The intelligence of creativity

Raising academic standards alone will not solve the problems we face: it may compound them. To move forward we need a fresh understanding of intelligence, of human capacity and of the nature of creativity. Human intelligence is richer and more dynamic than we have been led to believe by formal academic education. Advances in the scientific studies of the brain are confirming that human intelligence is complex and multifaceted. We can think about the world and our experiences in terms of sight, in touch, in sound, in movement and in many other ways. This is why the world is full of music, dance, architecture, design, practical technology, relationships and values. Brain-scanning techniques show that even simple actions draw simultaneously on different functions and regions of the brain.

Human culture is as rich and diverse as it is because human intelligence is so complex and dynamic. We all have great natural capacities, but we all have them differently. There are not only two types of people, academic or non-academic. We all have distinctive profiles of intellectual abilities with different strengths in visual intelligences, in sound, in movement, in mathematical thinking and the rest. Academic education looks only for certain sorts of ability. Those who have it often have other abilities that are ignored: those who don't are likely to be seen as not intelligent at all. Highly able people are turned away from companies or lost in them because their education tells the wrong story. If we're serious about developing human resources, the first step is to recognise how diverse and individual those resources are. This is the real road to realising creative potential.

Strategies for success

There is a problem with creativity. Companies and governments are very keen to promote it, but they're not sure what it is or who has it. Some politicians have a different problem. They obviously suspect that too much creativity in education may have been the reason that standards fell in the first place. Many of these anxieties are rooted in misconceptions about creativity. Often it is associated only with particular sorts of activities, especially the arts; or with particular sorts of people, the 'creatives' in companies, or those whose appearance or behaviour is unconventional. It is thought of as something people have or don't have, like brown eyes. It is often linked with being uninhibited and with free expression. The truth is that creativity is not a separate part of the brain that lights up only in certain people or during particular activities. Creativity is possible in science, in technology, in management, in business, in music, in any activity that engages human intelligence. People are not creative in general but in doing something concrete. Different people have different creative strengths according to the pattern of their intelligences. For some it will be music, or mathematics, or working with clay, or software, or images or with people. Real creativity comes from finding your medium, from being in your element. When people find their medium, they discover their real creative strengths and come into their own. Genuine creativity is not only a matter of letting go but of holding on.

Feeling better

There has been a lot of interest in the idea of emotional intelligence. Many people are not in touch with their emotions and feel incapable of expressing their feelings. The results everywhere are palpable and cata-strophic. In part, this is the legacy of the academic illusion. Conventional education separates intelligence from feeling, and concentrates only on particular aspects of the first. This is why being highly educated is no guarantee of emotional intelligence. Yet there is an intimate relationship between knowing and feeling: how we feel is directly related to what we know and think. Creativity is not a purely intellectual process. It is enriched by other capacities and in particular by feelings, intuition and by a playful imagination. The term 'flow' has been used to describe peak creative performances. These are times when we are immersed in something that completely engages our creative capabilities and draws equally from our knowledge, feelings and intuitive powers.

We need languages of feeling to express these perceptions, and this is one of the functions of the arts – of music, dance, poetry, drama and the rest – and one of the reasons for needing a new balance in the way we educate and train people. Arts techniques can be powerful ways of unlocking creative capacities and of engaging the whole person.

A culture of creativity

Creativity is related to culture. Cultural conditions can kindle or kill cre-ativity. We do not have creative ideas in a vacuum. Individual creativity is stimulated by the work, ideas and achievements of other people. We stand on the shoulders of others to see further. This is true in all fields, in business, science, sport, music, design, fashion, whatever. Human intelligence is creative in a profound sense. Thinking and feeling are not simply about seeing the world as it is, but of having ideas about it, of interpreting experience to give it meaning. Different communities live differently according to the ideas they have and the meanings they see. In a literal sense, we create the worlds we live in. But we can also recreate them. The great revolutions in human history have often been deto-nated by new ideas: by new ways of seeing that have shattered old cer-tainties. This is the essential process of cultural change and it can be deeply unsettling. Creative insights often occur by making connections between ideas or experiences that were previously unconnected. Just as intelligence in a single mind is interactive, creativity is often interdisci-plinary. This is why the best creative teams often contain specialists in different fields. This has serious implications for the culture of organisations that want to promote creative development.

There are two related tasks. First, to unlock the creative abilities in each individual. We all have creative abilities and we all have them differently. Creativity is not a single aspect of intelligence that only emerges in particular activities, in the arts for example. It is a systemic function of intelligence that can emerge wherever our intelligence is engaged. Creativity is a dynamic process that draws on many different areas of a person's experience and intelligence. We need to look at what it is in companies and organisations that blocks individual creativity. But this is only half the job. Creativity and innovation must be harnessed and not just released. Creativity is not purely an individual performance. It arises out of our interactions with ideas and achievements of other people. It is a cultural process. Creativity prospers best under particular conditions, especially where there is a flow of ideas between people who have different sorts of expertise. It requires an atmosphere where risk-taking and experimentation are encouraged rather than stifled. Just as individual creativity draws from many different skills and expertise in a single mind, corporate creativity draws on the skills and expertise across organisations. Creativity flourishes when there is a systemic strategy to promote it. The cultural environment should be modelled on the dynamics of intelligence. Many organisations stifle creativity in the structures they inhabit and the ethos they promote. If ideas are discouraged or ignored, the creative impulse does one of two things. It deserts or subverts the organisation. Creativity can work for you or against you.

Upstream downstream

In 1997 I was asked by the UK Government to chair a national task group on creativity, the economy and education. The National Advisory Committee on Creative and Cultural Education brought together leading business people, educators, artists and scientists. It worked across disciplinary boundaries and drew from many different professional backgrounds. The resulting report, *All Our Futures: Creativity Culture and Education,* was published in the summer of 1999. It drew a powerful response from business and from education. Over 100,000 copies of a summary of the report have been distributed by a wide range of commercial and public organisations. Before and since working on that report, I have worked with organisations in many different parts of the world on the issues that I set out in this book.[1] These are issues that matter deeply to people both personally and professionally. In *Out of Our Minds* I look at the origins of these concerns and at the wider contexts in which they are best understood and resolved.

In outline

This book is about issues that affect us all deeply. It's an ambitious book for its size, and ranges over a wide landscape of issues and ideas. It touches on economic globalisation and the revolutionary challenges facing business and work. It looks at the even more extraordinary developments in science and technologies that will make the changes we've seen so far seem primitive by comparison. It looks at how we educate people now and at the ideas about intelligence and human ability on which these systems are based. And it argues that there is a disastrous mistake at the heart of all of this. This range of coverage is necessary because I want to offer an overview of the nature and origins of a set of urgent problems we all face and of their possible solutions. Whatever strength this book has is in offering this big picture. Inevitably this is its potential weakness too because every chapter calls for a specialist book to work through the details. But here my concern is less with the detail and more with the major currents and crosscurrents that are driving forward the issues I want to talk about.

- *Chapter One* looks at the turbulent changes that are creating a widening gap between education and the needs of individuals, companies and communities. It argues that this revolution has hardly begun. Technological change is accelerating at an enormous rate. The changes we have experienced so far may be as nothing compared with what is to come.
- In *Chapter Two* I ask why education systems have become so obsessed with particular forms of academic ability. I look at the origins of this preoccupation and argue that its benefits are now being overwhelmed by the divisions it has helped to create between people and within our own conceptions of ourselves.
- There are far-reaching advances in our understanding of intelligence and human capacity. Many of these are being driven forward by developments in brain research. *Chapter Three* summarises some of

these insights and how they can enhance our understanding of creativity and human resources.

- In *Chapter Four* I look at the meaning of creativity and at the conditions under which it can thrive or be stifled. One of the legacies of academicism is the exile of feeling from education. Reconnecting feeling and intellect is vital for the development of human resources and for the promotion of creativity.
- *Chapter Five* looks at what is involved. Creative development does not take place in a vacuum. It feeds from and into the cultural context in which individuals work.
- In *Chapter Six* I look at the relationships between individual creative creativity and the cultural context and at the implications for creating a culture of creativity in organisations.
- *Chapter Seven* sets out key principles for developing and harnessing creative abilities in organisations and communities. It also draws these various arguments together into proposals for dealing with the upstream problem, the balance and priorities of formal and informal education systems.

Camping on common ground

For more than 25 years I have worked with people at all levels of education and in many parts of the world. I have worked with people in schools, colleges, universities, community groups, adult education and workers' education associations, and in all sorts of disciplines across the arts, sciences and humanities. I've worked with companies and commercial organisations: from multinational finance houses to information-technology organisations, e-commerce to traditional manufacturing, engineering and service organisations. In my experience there are many common concerns and interests across these groups. They also share a deep anxiety about the misconceptions that other people have about their work. Business wonders why education isn't producing the thoughtful, creative, self-confident people they urgently need. Yet many business people cling to an uncritical belief in the supreme importance of academic education.

The problems that organisations face are immediate; there are immediate things that can be done to address them and I say what they are. But the long-term solution lies upstream in the education system. This is now dominated by a narrow view of academic education that overlooks the greater part of young people's intellectual capacities just as it did yours. In the interests of raising standards, schools and universities are increasingly encased in standard testing regimes that inhibit teachers themselves from promoting creative development. In a profoundly ironic way, many political initiatives to raise standards in education are making matters worse. It is in the short- and long-term interests of companies and organisations of all sorts to take a direct practical interest in the development of education, locally and nationally, since much of what is going on is meant to be in their interests.

People in education want to pursue a more sophisticated agenda but feel hemmed in and often demoralised by political pressures to raise particular standards. Politicians say that this pressure comes from business and is essential to national economic survival. The popular press promotes a tireless antagonism between traditional and progressive teaching methods and campaigns against liberal education. They know that parents are sleepless with worry about the quality of education that their children are receiving. Yet in my experience parents, and I am one, often want a much broader and more sensitive style of education for their own children than politicians seem to promote for everyone else. This is why those who can afford to do so are taking their children out of state education to the independent sector. These schools can take a different approach.

All of these groups do have common interests. Governments pour huge amounts of money into education on the basis that it is vital to national economic development. Parents also assume that education will help their children to find work and become economically independent. We also want other things from education. At best, businesses want people who are literate, numerate, who can analyse information and ideas; who can generate new ideas of their own and help to implement them; who can communicate clearly and confidently and work well with other people. They want education to provide such people but too often they think it doesn't and they pay for education programmes of their own to make up the difference. Educators want to provide a balanced education that draws on their own creative energies as teachers and love for their own disciplines. Too often they feel they can't do any of this because of the pressures from central government, poor facilities and the increasing disaffection of students. Parents also want education to develop their children's best abilities and to help them lead lives that have purpose and enjoyment. This is what most learners want for themselves. For all these reasons, education could not be a higher priority. This is why governments pour such huge resources into it. But the problems of dissatisfaction seem to be deepening as the gap in expectations between all of these groups continues to widen.

Out of our minds?

I have called this book *Out of our Minds* for three reasons. First, human intelligence is uniquely creative. We live in a world constructed by the ideas, beliefs and values that are the product of human intelligence. The worlds we live in are created out of our minds as much as from the natural environment. Second, realising our creative potential is literally a question of finding our medium, of being in our element. Education should help us to do this, but too often it does not. This is because of the preoccupation with certain sorts of intellectual skills. In this sense, too many people are displaced from their own true capacities. They do not realise their potential because they do not know what it is. They are out of their element and out of their minds in that specific sense. Third, there is a kind of trance-like mania in the present direction of educational policy. In place of a reasoned debate about the strategies that are needed to face these extraordinary changes, there is an insistent mantra that we must raise traditional academic standards. These standards were designed for other times and for other purposes. We will not navigate through the complex environment of the future by peering relentlessly into a rear view mirror. To pursue this course we would be out of our minds in a more literal sense.

Ken Robinson

Chapter One

BURSTING THE BANKS

'By mid-century, computers will be linked directly into our nervous systems via nanotechnology, which is so small it could connect to every neuron in our brains. By about 2040, there will be a backup of our brains in a computer somewhere, so that when you die it won't be a major career problem.'

Ian Pearson[2]

Introduction

Technological innovations are driving economic and social change at a faster rate than ever before. In the 250 years or so since the Industrial Revolution began, the world has been transformed in every way. But the changes we have seen may be as nothing compared with those to come. We are in a deepening revolution in the work people do, who works and for how long, how we relate to each other and how we conceive our own intelligence and abilities. The most extraordinary developments may yet come from the merging of information technologies and human intelligence. These radical transformations call for radical strategies in how we think of and develop human resources. This chapter sketches in the changes that are in prospect, and the underlying crisis in how we are currently tackling the development of creativity and innovation.

The war for talent

Organisations are fighting a war for talent, according to recent studies by Andersen Consulting and the Institute of Management.[3] Up to 90 per cent of the chief executives in the survey said that attracting and retaining talented individuals was their major priority. Better talent is worth fighting for, according to a major report by McKinsey.[4] The report argues that at senior levels of an organisation, the ability to adapt, to make decisions quickly in situations of high uncertainty and to steer through change is critical. But at a time when the need for superior talent is increasing, the big US companies are finding it more and more difficult to attract and retain key people. Executives point to a worsening shortage of the people needed to run divisions and manage critical functions, let alone lead companies. McKinsey researched 77 large US companies in a variety of industries and worked with their human resources departments to understand their talent-building philosophies, practices and challenges. The research surveyed nearly 400 corporate offices and 6000 executives in the 'top 200' ranks in these companies. It also drew on case studies of 20 companies widely regarded as being rich in talent. The research concluded with a warning to corporate America that companies are about to be engaged in a war for senior executive talent that will remain a defining characteristic of the competitive landscape for decades to come. Yet most are ill-prepared and even the best are vulnerable.

There is a massive gap between the skills and abilities that business needs and those that are available in the workforce. Three-quarters of corporate officers said their companies had insufficient talent sometimes; all were chronically short of talent across the board. This shortage has put a new emphasis on the importance of lifelong learning. But too few employees have much trust in the provision by employers of opportunities in continuing education. Most organisations take a short-term view of training needs. Only a third of employers provide training beyond the job. In a rapidly changing environment there is little time and energy for training. Employers constantly fear that their best talent will be poached by other companies. This makes them wary of investing in developing their own talent since they fear it will primarily benefit their competitors. Consequently, staff turnover is often high and vacant posts are replenished with outside talent. To win the war for talent, 'most companies choose to develop more and more powerful recruitment and retention mechanisms to get the "right people" on board and identify the best performers.' One result is a bonanza for headhunters. In the United States, the revenues of headhunting firms have grown twice as fast as GDP during the past five years.

'The problem with the short-term model is that it does nothing to prevent the exodus of the rest – those whose talents are undeveloped. It assumes a world with an unlimited supply of talent, talent that does not mind working in businesses where development is not deemed a priority. Fighting the talent war with the outside world is covering up our failure in terms of people development.'

Javier Bajer (The Talent Foundation)

McKinsey concluded that part of the cause may be cyclical, the result of a strong economy at the peak of its cycle. But what should keep CEOs awake at night 'is a number of trends that threaten a wide-ranging shortage in talent over the next five years.'

- *Growing complexity.* A more complex economy demands more sophisticated talent with global acumen, multicultural fluency, technological literacy, entrepreneurial skills, and the ability to manage 'increasingly delayered, disaggregated organisations'.
- *Growing competition.* The emergence of efficient capital markets in the United States has enabled the rise of many small and medium-sized companies that are increasingly targeting the same people sought by large companies. Small companies exert a powerful pull across the whole executive spectrum, 'offering opportunities for impact and wealth that few large firms can match'.
- *Growing mobility.* Ten years ago a high-performer might have changed employers just once or twice in full career. According to 50 senior executive search professionals, the average executive today will work in five companies; in another ten years it may be seven.
- *A dwindling supply.* Until now the executive population has grown roughly in line with GDP. An economic growth rate of 2% for 15 years would increase demand for executives by about a third. But supply is moving in the opposite direction: the number of 35–44-year-olds in the United States will decline by 15 per cent between 2000 and 2015. 'Moreover no significant countervailing trends are apparent: women are no longer surging into the workforce, white-collar productivity

improvements have flattened, immigration levels are stable and executives are not prolonging their careers.'

According to McKinsey, a war that was once conducted as a sequence of set-piece recruiting battles is transforming itself into an endless series of skirmishes as companies find their best people and in particular their future senior executives under constant attack.

McKinsey suggests that executive talent has been the most under-managed corporate asset for the past two decades. Companies that manage their physical and financial assets with rigour and sophistication have not made their people a priority in the same way. Only 23% of some 6000 executives surveyed strongly agree that their companies attract highly talented people and just 10% that they retain almost all the high-performers. Perhaps more alarmingly, only 16% think their companies even know who their high-performers are, and only 3% said their companies develop effectively and move low performers on quickly. For McKinsey the moral is straightforward:

> 'You can win the war for talent but first you must elevate talent management to a burning corporate priority. Then to attract and retain the people you need, you must create and perpetually refine an employee value proposition: senior management's answer to why a smart, energetic, ambitious individual would want to come and work with you rather than with the team next door. That done, you must turn your attention to how you're going to recruit great talent and finally develop, develop, develop!'

Developing people's natural talents and abilities is the major theme of this book. We will come to the underlying problems shortly and to some of the solutions as we go on. But first, why is it with such massive national resources being poured into education and training, with the highest participation rates in all developed countries, and with standards apparently heading skywards, that there is still a profound abyss between what employers are looking for and what education is providing? That there is an abyss is now beyond question.

Into the abyss

As I write, there are 15 million people registered as unemployed in the European Union. Yet there are estimated to be millions of jobs unfilled because of a lack of qualified applicants. In a survey of the skills gap in the European economy, *Time* magazine concluded that:

'The best encapsulation of the old world labour plight comes not from Marx but from the English poet Samuel Taylor Coleridge, "Water, water, everywhere, nor any drop to drink." '

Most experts agreed, it went on, that Europe's jobs dilemma is grounded in an inflexible education system, high labour taxes and barriers to mobility. The chronically high number of jobless, roughly half of whom have been out of work for more than a year, is just part of the story.

' "There are twice as many people in Europe who would work, if work were available, as there are people currently recorded as unemployed", the European Employment Commissioner pointed out recently. There is no technological fix for closing the jobs gap. Chip capacity may double every 18 months, but there's no Moore's Law for Labour, in Europe or elsewhere.'

James Graff, Time *magazine*

As in the rest of the world, leaders in Europe have begun to recognise the vital need to put the vast potential to use. But how?

The world's biggest business

In the next 30 years, more people will be gaining formal qualifications through education and training than since the beginning of history. Education and training are now amongst the world's biggest businesses, accounting for more than six per cent of world GDP. There is an accelerating demand for educational qualifications of every sort. There are two reasons. First, the nature of work is being transformed by new technologies. As ideas become the main commodity in the new information age, there is a growing need for people to work with their minds rather than their hands: for intellectual rather than manual labour. The other factor is population growth. In 1960 the population of the world was three bil-lion. In 1999 it was six billion: it had doubled in 39 years. By 2013 it will be seven billion and growing fast. Populations are not growing evenly; this is an issue of some importance that we'll come back to. In Europe and America for example, many families now have only one or two chil-dren and population growth is slowing. Future patterns of population growth can't be certain. What is certain is that in global economies that are increasingly dominated by intellectual labour, education is going to be critical to the ability of individuals, families and of nations to sustain themselves.

Most countries have a dual strategy. The first is to increase the amount of education that goes on. Governments are right to do this. Now and in the future, more and more people will live by what they know; and what they need to know is changing every day. The second strategy is to raise standards. This seems sensible too. Education standards should be high and it is obviously a good idea to raise them. There's no point in lower-ing them. But standards of what and why? The essential problem is that many governments and organisations seem to think that the best way to prepare for the future is to do better what we did in the past – just to do more of it and to a higher standard. The fact is we have to do something else.

You're going the wrong way

When I was 14, I was told at school that I had a problem. I was sent to see the head teacher. The problem was my choice of subject option. I wanted to do art and German. 'Well you do have a problem, Robinson', he said. 'The fact is you can't do art and German.' I was baffled. I'd seen films about Germany and there seemed to be pictures everywhere. 'No,' he said, 'you can't do art and German here in this school. They clash on the timetable.' I asked him what I should do. 'If I were you,' he said, 'I should do German.' I asked him why, and he said, 'It will be more useful.' I found this intriguing and still do. I'd have understood if he'd said German would be more interesting; that I had an obvious feel for languages, or that it would suit me better. But why is German more useful than art? I know it is useful, especially in Germany. Languages are useful but is art not? Is it useless? For generations, children have been steered through school by this kind of advice. About the age of 14, they are eased away from some subjects and toward others on the ground of utility. Where has this idea of utility come from, and why does the school curriculum usually fall into two groups of subjects: the useful and the useless? Languages, maths, science and technology are useful; history, geography, art, music and drama are not. This is a very common pattern.

The Council of Europe is an intergovernmental organisation based in Strasbourg. It works with 48 member states across Europe including many of the former Soviet Bloc countries and all of the Western European states. In 1995, as part of a project that I directed for the Council of Europe, I surveyed education systems in 22 countries. Someone has to do this sort of thing. There were many differences in education in these countries and some striking similarities. In all countries the arts are on the edges of the school curriculum, in the useless rather than the useful band. Most national school systems include some art and music: very few teach drama and hardly any provide dance lessons in the formal school curriculum. This pattern is repeated in North America, Canada and in many parts of the Far East and Australasia and in fact in most systems based on Western principles. The drive to raise standards is squeezing the arts even further. Whatever standards are, most countries don't seem to think they have much to do with what the arts teach. And yet young people love the arts and enjoy them. So why are they so often talked out of them at school? Why are other subjects thought to be so much more useful? Useful to what and why? It's critical to understand the answer to this question.

The old model

All national systems of education are based on two underlying models. There is always an *economic* model and an *intellectual* model and there is assumed to be a relationship between the two. In western systems of education, and that now means much of the world, the underlying economic model is *industrialism;* and the intellectual model that supports it is *academicism.* The problem we now face is that this economic model is outmoded and the intellectual model is completely inadequate. All attempts to improve education by expanding it or by raising standards will fail if these two sets of assumptions are not completely reconstructed.

We take it for granted now that national governments should provide an education system that is funded and regulated by law. It seems obvious that all young people should go to school at least until they're 16 and that some will go on to college or university. But the whole apparatus of state education is relatively new. It was only in the 19th century that governments took a serious interest in education and only in the 20th century that it has become established in many countries as a right.[5] In Europe and the United States these systems of education were designed to meet the labour needs of the industrial economy. This was based on manufacturing, steel production, engineering and the related trades including coal mining and shipbuilding. For this, they needed a workforce that was roughly 80% manual and 20% professional and managerial. This assumption underpinned the whole structure of schooling and higher education.

In Britain, the 1944 Education Act set up three types of school: grammar, secondary modern and technical. The grammar schools were to educate the 20 per cent: the prospective doctors, teachers, lawyers, accountants, civil servants and managers of post-war Britain. It was assumed that these would need a rigorous academic education and that's what the grammar schools were intended to provide. Those sent to the secondary modern schools were destined for manual work. They were given an education that was really a watered-down version of the grammar school curriculum. Many European countries made similar sorts of provision. The assumption was clear-cut and accepted. If a person worked hard at school and gained good academic qualifications, and especially if they went to university, they were assured of secure, lifelong employment in a professional or office job. For over 100 years this narrative has been true and the system has worked well for those who successfully followed its rules. It is not working any more. The reason is the extraordinary nature of technological and economic change. We are caught up in a new economic revolution. And it has hardly begun. Education and training are meant to be the long-term answer for all of those asking how they are to survive the coming turbulence. But they will not provide the answer while we continue to misunderstand the question that this new revolution is presenting.

One small step?

In the late 1990s, there was a craze for Furbies, small furry toys with an onboard computer that could be taught to repeat phrases. These toys sold for £30 in high-street shops. In computing terms Furbies contained four times the computing power and 30 times the memory of the 1969 Apollo Moonlander, the space vehicle from which Neil Armstrong took his small step for man and his huge leap for mankind. Less dignified for a moon landing, but much more powerful and infinitely cheaper. If you'd bought a home computer in 1950 it would have taken up the entire living room. This was one reason people didn't buy them. A second was the cost. Even a basic computer would have cost hundreds of thousands of pounds – another disincentive. Governments and some companies could afford computers but few families could. Now home computers are everywhere. They sit on your desk top or kitchen table, are hugely more powerful than the early computers and most people on an average income can afford one. The pace of developments in computer technology over the past 50 years has been breathtaking. If the technology of motor cars had developed at the same rate, the average family car would be very different. It could travel at six times the speed of sound. It would be capable of about 1000 miles per gallon and it would cost you about 80p. I imagine you'd get one. You'd just have to be careful on the accelerator. The developments in computing illustrate two fundamental themes. First, what is distinctive about our times is not change itself but the nature of change. Second, the technological revolution is only just beginning.

Going headlong

In 1974 Alvin Toffler published his book *Future Shock*. The idea of culture shock is well known to psychologists. It can happen to people who suddenly find themselves in an environment where all their normal reference points – language, values, food, clothes, social rituals – are gone. Political refugees and economic migrants can experience culture shock when they move to a completely new country. This experience can be profoundly disorienting and can lead in extreme cases to psychosis. Toffler saw a similar global phenomenon in the effects of rapid social change promoted by technology. He argued that being propelled too quickly into an unfamiliar future could have the same traumatic effects on people. The issue was not the fact of change. Change is a constant factor in human history. The distinctive feature of change in our own times is the rate and scale of it. Take two examples: transport and writing systems.

> 'We have in our time released a totally new social force – a stream of change so accelerated that it influences our sense of time, revolutionises the tempo of daily life, and affects the very way we feel the world around us. We no longer feel life as people did in the past. And this is the ultimate difference, the distinction that separates the truly contemporary person from all others. For this acceleration lies behind the impermanence, the transience, that penetrates and tinctures our consciousness, radically affecting the way we relate to other people, to things, to the entire universe of ideas, art and values.'
>
> *Alvin Toffler*

Getting around

I used to live in England in a village called Snitterfield, near Stratford-upon-Avon. This is where William Shakespeare's father, John Shakespeare, was born. Until he was 34 years old he hadn't ventured far beyond the village. He then decided to leave Snitterfield to seek his fortune in Stratford. This is three miles away. It's almost impossible to grasp the differences in his view of the world compared with ours 500 years later. Business travellers now routinely fly club class across oceans and continents to attend two or three meetings and then head home for the weekend. But this change hasn't happened in 500 years, more like 100. In the Middle Ages, social change was snail-like by comparison. John Shakespeare's life was probably little different from his parents', grandparents' or great grandparents'.

My father was born in 1914. He spent most of his life in Liverpool and never left the UK. I was born in 1950. I've been to most countries in Europe, the Far East and many parts of the United States and of Australia, for work or pleasure. In the 1950s, I thought of my father's childhood in the 1920s as a medieval period: no television, few cars, steam trains, few telephones, grand steam ocean liners and no air travel to speak of. My own children have a similarly pitying view of my child-hood in the 1950s and 1960s: only two television channels both in black and white, no video, no computer games, no mobile phones, Walkmen, McDonald's or Internet. By the age of 12 they had been to more countries than I had visited at the age of 40. Their world is inconceivably different from my father's childhood and an epoch away from his life. All in less than 80 years. According to a recent estimate:

- in 1950, the average person travelled about 5 miles per day;
- in 2000 the average person travelled about 30 miles per day; and
- in 2020 the average person will travel about 60 miles per day.

To get some sense of the pace of change, imagine the past 3000 years as the face of a clock with each of the sixty minutes representing a period of fifty years. Until three minutes ago, the history of transport was domi-nated by the horse, the wheel and the sail. In the late 18th century, James Watt refined the steam engine. This changed everything. It was a major tremor in the social earthquake of the Industrial Revolution. The steam engine vastly increased the speed and power of transport by road and sea and it made possible the development of railways, the arterial system of the early industrial world. The steam engine made possible vast movements of humanity at speeds never before thought possible. Since then, the curve of change has climbed almost vertically:

- 3 minutes ago the internal combustion engine;
- 2 minutes ago the motor car;
- 90 seconds ago the jet engine;
- 1 minute ago rocket propulsion;
- 50 seconds ago space travel; and
- 10 seconds ago the reusable space shuttle.

In 1999, another 550,000 cars were added to the national fleet in the United Kingdom. These would represent a 300-mile queue of parked cars six lanes wide. There have been many benefits in the growth of mobility. There have also been negative consequences. These include the fear parents have of letting children play even in their own neigh-bourhoods. When I was a young child, my parents happily let me play in the local park about half a mile from our home. I would play there all afternoon with friends and my brothers and sister often returning hours later on my own. There was no fear that anything disastrous would befall me. Nowadays parents are increasingly frightened of dangers to their children and drive them everywhere and keep them under almost constant surveillance. In 1950 people knew who their neighbours were, not only on either side but in the whole community. Now all communities are permeable and often transitory. These changes in mobility are matched by the increasing speed of communication, and the sheer volume of information available to us.

Getting the message

A well-known British journalist was reminiscing about his early days in radio news. He joined the BBC in the 1930s at a time when there was no regular news bulletin. In his first week, a bulletin was scheduled and he arrived at the studio to watch it being broadcast. The presenter sat at the microphone and waited until the time signal had finished. He then announced sombrely: 'This is the BBC Home Service from London. There is no news.' The view of the times was that news would be broadcast if anything happened to warrant it. Compare this with our own saturated processes of news-reporting 24 hours a day on a multitude of channels and media. This is not because there is more going on in the world in the 21st century than there was in the middle of the 20th century. There is a ferociously hungry news industry which has developed its own momentum for breaking and if necessary generating news stories around the clock. All of this adds to a general sense of events and crisis which permeates 21st century culture.

Human beings have had access to writing systems of various sorts for at least 3000 years. Imagine that whole period in terms of the 60 minutes on a clock face with each minute equivalent to fifty years. For most of the past 3000 years writing systems hardly changed at all. People communicated with handmade marks on surfaces, using pens on paper, chisels on stone or pigment on boards. Written documents had to be copied by hand or they existed in single copies. Only a privileged few had access to them and only those few needed to be able to read.

About 550 years ago – 11 minutes ago on our clock – Gutenberg invented the printing press. This invention changed everything. Suddenly it was possible for documents to be reproduced in volume and distributed far and wide. Printing opened up the world of ideas to everyone, and generated a universal appetite for literacy. It had vast consequences for religion, politics and culture. This was a pivotal moment in the history of communication. Since then the process of change has gathered at a furious pace. Think of the major innovations in communication in the past 200 years, and how the gap between them has shortened:

- 3 minutes ago Morse Code;
- 2½ minutes ago the telephone;
- 2 minutes ago the radio;
- 90 seconds ago the television;
- 1 minute ago the fax;
- 25 seconds ago the personal computer;
- 12 seconds ago the Internet; and
- 6 seconds ago the mobile phone.

The Internet and mobile phone have revolutionised communications worldwide. The Internet is the most powerful and pervasive communication system every devised. For most of us, it didn't exist until 5 years ago. In 1997 there were 40 million Internet users in the United States and an estimated 10 million users in Asia. In 2000 there were 100 million users in the United States compared with 45 million in Asia. On current estimates, the number of Asian users will match US users early in the decade with an estimated 160 million users each. Thereafter, Asia is set to overtake the US at a rapid rate.

> 'Television will never be a serious competitor for radio because people must sit and keep their eyes glued on a screen. The average American family doesn't have time for it.'
> New York Times *at the 1939 World's Fair*

The Internet is an organism with millions upon millions of connections, with millions more being added daily at an ever-faster rate. The connection systems are arranged in patterns that bear more than a striking resemblance to dendritic groupings or ganglia. So the Internet can be seen as a physical model of neural networks. In the brain, the synapses that fire most often have the most robust response. The Internet has a similar kind of behaviour.[6] When Alvin Toffler was developing his apocalyptic views on the rate of social change, the personal computer hadn't even been invented, let alone the Internet. He wrote *Future Shock* on a manual typewriter. Most of the formative technologies of the early 21st century came into being in the last 15 years of the 20th century – 20 seconds on our clock face.

These are just two examples of the exponential rate of change in our own times, change that is driven by technological innovation. With these innovations have come vast and complex cultural changes in how we think, what we believe, how we work and relate to each other. But the technological revolution is far from over. In some ways, we have seen nothing yet. Let me take two examples that promise to transform the landscape of our lives in the 21st century beyond anything we have seen yet: nanotechnology and neuroscience.

Think small

Nanotechnology is the manipulation of very small things indeed. Nano-technologists are building machines by assembling individual atoms and molecules. To measure the vast distances of space, scientists use the light year, the distance that light travels in a year, or miles. I asked a professor of nanotechnology what they use to measure the unthinkably small distances of nanospace? He said it was the nanometre. This didn't help me very much. A nanometre is a billionth of a metre. Mathematically this is 10^{-9} metre or 0.000000001 metre. I understood the idea but couldn't visualise what it meant. I said, 'What is that roughly?' He thought for a moment and said, 'A nanometre is roughly the distance that a man's beard grows in one second.' I'd never thought about what beards does in a second but they must do something. It takes them all day to grow about a millimetre. They don't leap out of your face at eight o'clock in the morning. Beards are slow, languid things and our language reflects this. We do not say 'as quick as a beard' or 'as fast as a bristle'. We now have a way of grasping of how slow they are – about a nanometre a second.

Nanotechnology makes it feasible to shrink existing personal computers to the size of a wristwatch. Soon they could be worn on the body and be powered by the surface electricity of your skin. The problem is what to do with the monitor: you won't want the world's most advanced computer on your wrist and a large television strapped on your chest. One solution is retinal projectors. These have been developed particularly for the entertainment industry for use with virtual reality systems. They use small low level lasers and are worn on something like spectacle frames. They project the computer display directly onto the retina so that it is seen in your eye. A version of this technology is already in use in advanced aircraft systems such as the Stealth Bomber. Using these systems, pilots see the navigation displays from the on-board computers projected onto the inside of their visors. They are able to affect the direction of the aircraft by moving their eyes. You have to hope they don't sneeze in hostile airspace.

Nanotechnology is opening up extraordinary new horizons. It promises a sharp upward curve in computing and information systems. Nanotechnology makes possible a new phase of miniaturisation. The reason that computers don't now take up the whole living room is the past rate of miniaturisation. In 1940, the inside of a computer was full of bulky glass valves. In 1950 the transistor was invented and this helped to shrink the computer enormously. In 1970, the silicon chip was developed and computers shrank again. These inventions reduced the size of computers, but they also vastly increased their speed and power. Children now have toys in their bedrooms that have more computing power than the 1960s mainframes. It has been estimated that each year something in the order of 10^{17} microchips are being manufactured. This is roughly equivalent to the world population of ants. This extraordinary rate of production mirrors the vast range of applications for which microchips are now being used. The extreme miniaturisation of computer systems will revolutionise how and why we use them. Already in development are intelligent fridges, microwaves, cars and personal health monitors.

Key moments in the development of computing

1939 First electronic digital computer, created at Iowa State University.

1957 US Department of Defense forms the Advanced Research Projects Agency (ARPA) in response to the launch by the USSR of Sputniks I and II.

1958 ARPA's ARPANET lays foundations of Internet. Telstar relays a television signal. 200 million people watch the first live international television show.

1965 Thomas Merrill and Lawrence Roberts set up the first phone link between two computers, one in California, one in Massachusetts.

1969 Apollo 11 lands on the moon.

1972 First email program created.

1974 The term 'Internet' first used by Vint Cerf from Stanford and Bob Kahn from DARPA (formerly ARPA)

1975 The Altair, a personal computer in kit form goes on sale and spawns home-computing culture. Bill Gates (19) and Paul Allen write Altair BASIC language then form Microsoft.

1976 College dropout Steve Wozniak builds the Apple I in his spare time with Altair employee Steve Jobs.

1981 IBM enters home-computing market and sells 136,001 in first 18 months. Operating system bought from Gates.

1983 Internet Activities Board created. Number of hosts (i.e. the computer systems linked to the Internet) passes 500. Microsoft Word launched.

1984 1000 Internet hosts.

1987 10,000 Internet hosts.

1989 100,000 Internet hosts.

1990 ARPANET is disbanded. Hypertext system emerges on Internet. British academic Tim Berners-Lee of CERN (the European Organisation for Nuclear Research in Geneva) creates first World Wide Web software based on concept of hypertext, allowing academics to research each other's documents internationally on the Net. Microchips that can store 520,000 characters on a sliver of silicon 15 mm by 5 mm are invented in Japan.

1992 Internet hosts exceed 1 million.

1993 Internet hosts exceed 2 million.

1994 Annual Web growth rate of 341,634 per cent.

1996 Internet hosts exceed 9 million, rising to 13 million by July.

1997 Internet hosts exceed 16 million, rising to 20 million by July. Term 'e-commerce' enters into popular usage.

1998 America Online announces it will acquire Netscape Communications Corporation in a stock transaction valued at 4.2 billion dollars. UK banks begin to offer online banking services.

1999 Global number of Internet users exceeds 200 million.

(Information from the British Film Institute)

New applications will include wearable computers, which are woven into clothes, clipped to belts, slotted into jewellery and fashioned as goggles. Shirts could have sensors that monitor heartbeat and other vital signs via cuff links. Hints of serious ill health could be relayed from the shirt to the earrings that act as satellite transmitters to a doctor. A watch could fold out two arms as aerials allowing the timepiece to double as a mobile phone, with full paging, messaging and Internet access. Voice-activated necklaces have been developed that do a similar job and provide Internet radio services. Shoes could have smart gadgets inside that turn the action of walking or running into enough energy to power a wearable computer. They could also have a chip which tracks a child's location, relaying the information to its parents. If the child strayed away from a pre-programmed route while out shopping or on the way to school, a loudspeaker in the child's clothing would be activated and scold it in the voice of a parent.[7]

Think big

Nanotechnology is also opening new frontiers in the material sciences. In 1995, the British scientist Professor Sir Harry Kroto won the Nobel Prize for Chemistry for discovering the third form of carbon. This discovery has triggered an avalanche of research and development in material sciences that could change everything in engineering, aerospace, medicine and much else. The third form of carbon is a nanotube of graphite known as the C60 molecule. It is also known as the Buckminster Fullerene or Bucky Balls after the American architect Buckminster Fuller. Fuller made extensive use of geodesic shapes and structures which are similar to the structures of the C60 molecule. This molecule has remarkable qualities. It is 100 times stronger than steel, a tenth of the weight and it conducts electricity like a metal. If it can be produced in industrial quantities, the C60 has immense applications. It would make possible the construction of aeroplanes 20 or 50 times the present size and much more fuel-efficient. The present limitations are set by the strength and weight of existing steels and fibres. Buildings could be erected that go through the atmosphere and stay up: bridges could span the Grand Canyon or the English Channel. Motor cars and trains could be a fraction of their current weight with much greater fuel economies through the use of solar power.

Just think

A second new frontier is our understanding of the brain. The technologies of brain scanning have made it possible for the first time to study the processes of living brains. For generations, scientists have based their understanding of brain functions on dissecting dead brains on laboratory tables. There are some obvious drawbacks. Different theories have come and gone about the functions of different regions of the brain and about how the physical brain relates to human thought. Brain scanning allows the study of living brains. Neuroscientists are now looking in two related directions. Using so-called mind-mapping techniques, they are developing our understanding of the gross functions of the brain – what parts of the brain are used and in what combinations during different activities: in speech for example, or visual recognition of faces, listening to music, doing mathematics. They are also studying the processes of the brain at molecular level including the transfer of electrical charges at the neural synapses. These studies could lead to wholly new approaches in medicine, in psychology, in the design and use of drugs, and in the treatment of pain.

I'll come back to some of these issues in *Chapter Three*. They have immense significance for how we think about creativity, intelligence and about what it is to be human and conscious. There is an immediate point to make. It is that some of the most exciting and extraordinary implications of current research in these different fields – information systems, material sciences, and neuroscience – lie in the crossovers between them. Information systems are being revolutionised by innovations in nano-technology; neuroscience is also operating at nano level in exploring processes of thought and perception. It is now possible to conceive of information technologies modelled on the neural processes of the brain. A new generation of computers is being conceived that will be based not on digital codes and silicon but on organic processes and DNA: comput-ers that mimic human thought.

Ostman notes that artificially growing skin cultures are being pro-duced at New York University and research in the development of an organic artificial heart is taking place in several different locations. There have already been experiments in which a completely blind patient's optic nerve fibres were connected to a computer-driven dot matrix dis-play and the patient was able to see crude patterns. At Carnegie Mellon University in Pittsburgh, nano machines with rotor blades on the scale of human hair are being constructed as scrubbers to swim through veins and arteries cleaning out cholesterol and plaque deposits. According to Ostman, the next step could be machines that could actually think, reason and learn. Once we have mechanical components such as gears, levers, rackets, rollers and bearings and spring loaded actuators on a molecular

'Applications of nanotechnology range from molecular comput-ing, to shape changing alloys, to synthetic organic compounds, to custom gene construction, to ultra-miniaturised machinery. In medical applications, the implications for modifying the intercel-lular chemistry of almost any organ of the human body to cure dis-ease, prolong life, or to provide the potential for enhanced sensory and mental abilities, are almost beyond comprehension. The very boundaries of philosophical questions concerning where life ends and something else, yet to be defined, begins are at best soon to become a very fuzzy grey zone of definitions, as will the essence of intelligence as it is currently defined. But that's only the beginning, because right now power and influence in the world is based on the control of natural and industrial resources. Once nanotechnol-ogy makes it possible to synthesise any physical object cheaply and easily, our current economic systems will become obsolete. It would be difficult to envision a more encompassing realm of future development than nanotechnology.'

Charles Ostman

scale, it would be possible to produce ultra computers also on a molecular scale. A handful of different types of so-called molecular computing systems are being investigated, 'any one of which could suddenly and by several levels of magnitude drastically change the computing limitations we're struggling with today'.

It is estimated that within the next ten years the intelligence of machines could exceed that of humans. Within several decades, machines could exhibit the full range of human intellect, emotions and skilis, ranging from musical and other creative attitudes to physical movement. By 2019, 'a $1000 computer will at least match the processing power of the human brain.'[8] By 2029, the software for intelligence will have been largely mastered and the average personal computer will be equivalent to 1000 brains. If this happens, there will no longer be a clear distinction between human and machine. Computers, in the form of neural implants, are already being implanted directly into people's brains to counteract Parkinson's disease and tremors from multiples sclerosis. Cochlear implants are available to restore hearing. A retinal implant is being developed in the United States that is intended to provide at least some visual perception in blind individuals by replacing certain visual processing circuits of the brain. In 2020, neural implants could improve our sensory experiences, our memory and thinking.

As Kurzweil points out, the evolution of biological life and the evolution of technology have both followed the same pattern. They take a long time to get going, but advances build on one another and progress erupts at an increasingly furious pace: 'During the 19th century, technological progress was equal to that of the 10 centuries that came before it. Advancement in the first two decades of the 20th century matched that of the entire 19th century. Today significant technological transformations take just a few years. Computing technology is experiencing the same exponential growth.' The pattern of growth has been described as Moore's Law. Gordon Moore was a co-founder of Intel in the mid-1960s. He recognised that technologies were doubling the density of transistors on integrated circuit every 12 months. This meant computers were periodically doubling both in capacity and in speed per unit cost.

In the mid-1970s Moore revised his observation of doubling time to a more accurate estimate of about 24 months and that trend has persisted throughout the 1990s. After decades of devoted service, Moore's Law will have run its course around 2019. By that time transistors will be just a few atoms in width. The new computer architectures will continue the exponential growth of computing. For example, computing cubes are already being designed that will provide thousands of laser circuits, not just one as in today's computer chips. Computer speed per unit cost doubled every three years between 1910 and 1950 and every two years between 1950 and 1966 and is now doubling every year. It took 90 years to achieve the first $1000 computer capable of executing 1 million instructions per second (MIPS). Now we add an additional MIPS to a $1000 computer every day.[9]

Kurzweil estimates that by the third decade of the 21st century, we will be in a position to create complete, detailed maps of the computationally relevant features of the human brain, and to recreate these designs in advanced neural computers. We will provide a variety of bodies for our machines too, from virtual bodies in virtual reality to bodies comprising swarms of nanobots. Humanoid robots that walk and have lifelike facial expressions are already being developed in several laboratories in Tokyo.

'Before the next century is over, the law of accelerating returns tells us, earth's technology-creating species – us – will merge with our own technology. And when that happens we might ask: what is the difference between a human brain enhanced a millionfold by neural implants and a non-biological intelligence based on the reverse engineering of the human brain that is subsequently enhanced and expanded? An evolutionary process accelerates because it builds on its own means for further evolution. The intelligence that we are now creating in computers will soon exceed the intelligence of its creators.'

Ray Kurzweil

The interaction of genetics, neuroscience and information systems makes it feasible to think seriously about computer-enhanced intelligence. Scholarly papers are now being written about ways of extending human memory by implanting microprocessors into the brain. So if you have an important exam coming up you might in future be able to pop down to the shops and buy another 60 megabytes of RAM. Or it may be possible to have a language implant. Instead of spending five years learning French you can have it implanted in time for your summer holidays. This may sound far-fetched, but some version of it is already conceptually feasible. If someone had told you 15 years ago that you could communicate through your television with the Library of Congress, send instant letters, or design a building, or model a typhoon, you would have thought they were being ridiculous too. Now we take it for granted. The impossible yesterday is routine today.

I remember reading an article about a man in San Francisco who was launching a lawsuit demanding his constitutional right to be cloned. He clearly believed that as cloning was available he was entitled as a citizen and taxpayer to be reproduced in whatever numbers best suited him. It's easy to see the attraction of being available in duplicate or triplicate. It would be possible to attend several meetings simultaneously or not leave the house at all while travelling in various parts of the planet. Developments in genetics are throwing up profound issues in ethics that were inconceivable 50, 20, or even 10 years ago.

The real point is that science and technology are not self-contained. They affect everything. New technologies are affecting everything as they always have done, but in a way and at a rate that is without precedent. Think first of the effects on business and the economy.

New work for old

From pre-history to the present day, technological change has always gone hand in hand with economic and social change. Once again, technological change is transforming the work people do and how they do it. It has profound implications for who works and who doesn't, and for where they work and do not. For a number of years, the balance has been shifting from traditional forms of industrial and manual work to jobs that are based on information technology and providing services. In the past 15 years the economies of the developed world have shifted on their axis. Whereas the dominant global corporations used to be concerned with industry and manufacturing, the key companies today are in the fields of communications, information, entertainment, science and technology.

E-business

E-commerce and Internet trading have vast implications for established ways of doing business, for the structures of companies and markets. Internet trading has shattered the traditional structures of the financial services: of banks, insurance companies, stockbrokers and dealers. The huge growth in financial services in the 1980s and 90s was generated by a relatively small but highly paid labour force. This was made possible by the computerisation of the financial markets and the synchronisation of the global economies. Among the first casualties are the front-line sales forces of the financial sectors. Since the Big Bang in London in 1988, the financial services sector has been swept up in a revolution. Established banks have been swallowed up by international corporations, super-markets are offering financial services of their own, high-street branches have closed, Internet banking has become a reality, banks have become insurance and mortgage brokers. Along the way, many people have been made redundant and entirely new forms of financial services have arisen. All of this in less than 15 years. We now have a multifaceted finan-cial services sector that would have been unimaginable 20 years ago.

Lou Gerstner, Chief Executive of IBM, has estimated that companies will invest billions of dollars globally on e-business in the coming five years. Most of this will not be spent on hardware or software but on con-sultancy. McKinsey claimed to have more than 60 per cent of its London consultants employed on e-commerce projects in 2000. In 1998 it was less than 10 per cent. According to a *Times* report, traditional consultancies saw staff turnover rates rise rapidly in 2000 as people defected to dot-coms. Turnover in some companies was as high as 40%.

'At the graduate and MBA entry levels, consultancies have seen a sharp fall in their "offer to accept" ratios at leading universities and business schools. Professor David Reibstein, Associate Dean at the Wharton School, reports that one top-rank strategy consulting firm used to experience an 85% acceptance rate for offers made to MBAs from the school. In 1999 this rate fell to 60%. In 2000 it collapsed to 25%. At the London Business School, about 15% of the 2000 gradu-ating class joined an e-commerce company or start-up compared with less than 5% in 1998.'

The Times, *15 June 2000*

More venture capital in all categories was dispensed in the two years from 1998 to 2000 than in the previous ten. A great deal of this money was misplaced and lost. This was partly because in the frenzy to invest in the new forms of trading, many business people and investors alike forgot or overlooked some of the most basic principles of business. These included being able to guarantee that the goods promised would reach the person they were promised to within reasonable time and in good shape. Many Internet companies simply did not have the infrastructure to provide the services they offered. Many others were offering services that nobody really wanted to have provided.

According to *Fortune* magazine, venture capitalists spent the three years from 1997 to 2000 pouring money into companies that soon disappointed their expectations. In the late 1990s, they were:

'... tripping over themselves to get their hands on Web sites that sold sporting goods, gardening supplies, jewellery, cosmetics, banks, shoes, arts and crafts, watches, couches you name it. They jostled to get their investors' millions into sites that paid people to look at advertising, free services where you can plan your schedule, and bizarre Web confections such as the short-lived, self-proclaimed "leading provider of online barbecue supplies", whatever that means.'[10]

By 2000, the stock market loathed these companies and '99% of venture capitalists wouldn't even read their business plans, much less cough up money for them.' Venture capitalists invested $65 billion into Internet companies between January 1988 and July 2000, according to Venture One, a San Francisco research firm.

Along the way, some e-commerce organisations became extraordinarily valuable. Cisco Systems is a Bay area firm with 34,000 employees which supplies networking equipment for transmitting electronic signals on the Internet. In November 2000 its stock market value was $400 billion, even allowing for the previous decline in shares in technology companies. This made Cisco worth more than the combined value of all the world's car companies, steel makers, aluminium companies and aircraft manufacturers.

'According to Nat Schindler, Internet equity research analyst at Credit Suisse First Boston, total business-to-business economic activity worldwide in 2000 amounted to $47,000 billion. Of this, 65% or $30,000 billion will eventually be conducted electronically. The marketplaces will take 40% of that, amounting to $12,000 billion. If they charge fees of 3.5%, the market will amount to $400 billion a year. The result is a land rush to set up B2B marketplaces to stake out some part of this new commercial landscape.'

Financial Times, *October 2000*

The creative industries

One of the fastest-growing areas of the UK economy is the so-called creative industries. In 1988 a study was published on the economic importance of the arts in Britain. This marked an important shift in public and political perceptions about the arts. Traditionally the visual and performing arts had been seen as interesting but not useful, as recreational or leisure activities. The arts received public money, but this was seen as subsidy, as a loss leader so to speak. The 1988 study made an important new argument: that the arts make a significant contribution to the national economy and are serious forms of employment for very many people. In 1988 this contribution was estimated at six billion pounds per year to GDP. In 1998, the Government set up a creative industries task-force. The following year it published an assessment of the economic significance of this sector.[11] It defined the creative industries as including advertising, architecture, arts and antiques, crafts, design, fashion, film, leisure software, music, performing arts, publishing, software and computer services, television and radio.

In 1998 the government estimated that these creative industries had generated annual revenues of £60 billion, a tenfold increase in ten years. The communications revolution, increasing bandwidth and the advent of digital networks are creating new global markets, multiplying outlets and increasing consumer demand. These new forms of work are creating a demand for new sorts of skill and aptitude. Unlike many other industrial sectors, the creative industries continue to benefit from high growth rates, in part because they build on and interact with innovations in science and technology. In Britain, employment in the creative industries grew by 34% in a decade, against a background of almost no growth in employment in the economy as a whole.

This picture is comparable in the United States. There, the intellectual property sectors, whose value depends on their ability to generate new ideas rather than to manufacture commodities, are now the most powerful element in the US economy. The Intellectual Property Association in Washington has estimated these sectors to be worth currently $360 billion a year, making them more valuable than automobiles, agriculture or aerospace. They are growing at twice the rate of the economy as a whole, and generating jobs at three times the underlying rate. The intellectual property sector is even more significant when patents from science and technology are included: in pharmaceuticals, electronics, biotechnology, and information systems among others. All of these technologies are based on fundamental advances in the sciences and in engineering. They are creative fields of huge significance. The creative industries are labour-intensive and need many different types of specialist skill. Television and film production for example, draws on a variety of specialist roles in performance, in script writing, in camera and sound operation, in lighting, makeup, design, editing and postproduction. As the financial significance of this sector grows, so does its employment base. This is not true of the financial services.

Telecommunications

One of the fastest-growing global industries is telecommunications. Ten years ago, only a few enthusiasts could be bothered to walk around with a bulky mobile telephone. Since then, mobile phone technology has moved up an exponential curve of development. It is now one of the fastest-growing markets in Europe, the United States and Asia. Continuing developments in information technology will lead inevitably to a convergence of Internet access with mobile phone systems, and increase the penetration and flexibility of these technologies. This sector has also been subject to immense fluctuations in financial fortunes. Equipment suppliers have risen up on a tide of investment, only to find it ebb away as the major systems providers found their original estimates failed. The future fortunes of the telecommunications market are far from certain: what is certain is that they have changed beyond all recognition in a space of ten years and will do so again in the coming five. As information and communication technologies continue to evolve we can expect to see equally widespread changes in other established businesses including music, publishing and video outlets.

Population growth

Technological change is one reason for companies to look again at how they manage and develop human resources, and in particular the essential powers of creativity and adaptability. But there is another: the changing demography of world populations and of national work forces. Here again we are faced with an exponential curve of change. The global workforce is changing in size and shape. It took all of human history until the early 1800s for the world's population to reach the first billion. It took 130 years to reach the second billion in 1930, 30 years to add the third in 1960, 14 years to add the fourth in 1974 and 13 years to add the fifth in 1987. In 1999, the world's population reached 6 billion. This billion increase in 12 years was the most rapid increase ever. The United Nations medium projections show that another billion people will be added in just 14 years and that world population will be about 9.4 billion by 2050.

Most of the world's population growth is taking place in less developed countries. Currently, 84 million people are being added every year in less developed countries compared with only about 1.5 million in more developed countries. According to the UN, today's more developed country populations are projected to remain relatively constant throughout the next century, while less developed country populations are projected to keep growing.[12]

- China is the world's most populous nation with a 1998 population of 1.2 billion. Its population is increasing by 1% each year, assuming minimal migration. India has fewer inhabitants (989 million) but a higher annual growth rate of about 1.9%. India is likely to surpass China as the world's most populous country by the middle of the 21st century.
- In the 1990s, most of the world's fastest-growing countries were in the Middle East and Africa. Kuwait's 1998 population of 1.9 million grew by about 3.7% a year. At that rate the population will double in 19 years unless there is a significant decline in fertility or increase

in emigration. The population of the African continent is growing at 2.5%, yielding a doubling time of only 27 years.

- In contrast many countries are experiencing extremely slow growth and even natural decrease because death rates have risen above birth rates. Deaths exceeded births in 13 European countries including Russia, Germany and the Czech Republic in the late 1990s. In some countries net immigration provides the only population growth.
- The United States is the third most populous nation in the world, behind China and India. The US population increased by an estimated 2.5 million people during 1997. Legal and illegal migrants accounted for one quarter of population growth during the 1980s and about one-third of growth during the 1990s. According to the US Census Bureau projections, the US population could reach 394 million by 2050.

The changing patterns and demography of world population will have profound effects on the patterns of economic activity and trade.

The grey revolution

According to the Industrial Society[13] in the UK, by 2020 the number of working people under 50 will have dropped by 2 million, while the number over 50 will have increased by 2 million. Employers looking to their traditional source of labour – young workers – will find that the spring is running dry. Fortunately, the generation now passing 50 are not like their predecessors from generations past. They account for 80% of the nation's wealth, enjoy better health and are more inclined than the heavily mortgaged parents of young children to take on new challenges and adapt to new ways of working. This makes them highly effective new-economy workers. The report found that the grey revolution was already well underway. The over 50s were returning to work faster than the rest of the population as demand for their skills ratcheted up. From 1999 to 2000, the employment rate for women aged 50 and over increased at almost three times the rate for the workforce as a whole. In the four years from 1996 to 2000, the Australian economy created 360,000 full-time jobs and three-quarters went to workers aged 45 and over.

According to the Industrial Society, the British economy will fail if it does not make better use of the skills and wisdom of the over 50s. A recent report presented evidence from the dot-com sector to show that even youthful start-up companies in the new technology industries have started looking for older workers to provide the experience and strategic vision needed for survival. 'Declining birth rates mean that employers are going to have to become more creative if they want to access the knowledge workers they need. And that means abandoning the lazy prejudice of age discrimination', says the Society.

Home alone

The numbers of workers paid for work at home in the United States rose from 1.9 million in 1991 to 3.6 million in 1997.[14] Government-commissioned research in the United Kingdom published in November 2000 showed that 24% of men now work at home and a further 38% would like to do so. This is not because they want to spend more time with their families but because they believe they can better meet the demands of their jobs and be more effective away from the distractions of the workplace. Fewer women than men wanted to work from home, although 16% already do so and a further 33% would like to do so. The research also shows a huge demand for flexible working hours and a willingness on the part of employers to go along with these arrangements. According to a government spokesman:

'Working from home has advantages for companies and staff. There can be increases in efficiency and improvements in quality of life. Advances in new technology mean that it is now possible for more people to work from home than ever before.'

Seeing the future?

It is important to grasp the unpredictability of many technological and economic developments. Social and economic evolution rarely takes place in a straight and predictable line. If it did, the legions of pundits in newspapers and magazines would be redundant themselves. Progress is often refractory and recursive, as one innovation bounces awkwardly off another to create an unexpected effect. A good example of this is the fate of the widespread predictions of the paperless office.

The paperless office?

The development of the Internet, email and the word processor led to widespread, confident predictions about the paperless office. With these new electronic media, there would be no need for written communications to be sent on paper, or so it was said. In fact, the demand for office paper in total has grown on average by 8.1% each year since 1981. It is predicted to grow by at least 4–5 per cent until 2010 and even beyond. This overall increase conceals some intriguing underlying trends. There has been a relative decline in demand for copier paper. In Europe, between 1995 and 2000 the consumption of copier paper reduced by 11%. So what is driving the growth in office paper sales? There are two factors. The first is information. The amount of information available to the average office worker will, according to some reports, increase six-fold by the year 2010.

Toby Marchant, Managing Director of the Robert Horne Paper Company, notes that this insatiable appetite for information is coupled with a quantum leap in ease of access. There are around 11 million users of the Internet in the UK and that figure is increasing by about 10,000 a day.

'Although the percentage of information being printed is in sharp decline, this is more than compensated for by the fact that the amount of information available to us is doubling every two years. The net effect is growth in office papers of around 5% across Europe.'

Many people don't like reading complicated emails, and print them off to look at them later. Email speeds communication but it encourages a more thoughtless process of writing – what has been called a stream of unconsciousness. Word processors encourage repeated drafting and new levels of perfectionism that are creating an exponential demand for paper.

As Toby Marchant argues, underlying these patterns is a profound change in the way documents are produced. The old way was print and distribute, a way of working that was dominated by the photocopier and small officer printer. The new mode is distribution and print: 'This is the realm of the office printer and everyone has access to one of those. The world has gone from supporting 10,000 publishers to 100 million publishers and the figure rises every minute.' The paperless office is a clear fiction, although the products and applications and, most importantly, the customers for paper have changed radically. In 1997, the printer overtook the copier as the largest consumer of paper. By 2000 and by 2005 two-thirds of all paper in the office will go through the printer. The fate of the paperless office is just one example of the difficulty of predicting the effects of technological innovations on economic and social systems. So is the idea of the leisured society.

The leisured society

The new technologies are blurring the boundaries between home and work, business and pleasure. They are invasive and pervasive. The boundaries between office and home, work and play, the office and life, are dissolving into one long work shift. Most executives have computers at home and find themselves checking emails on the way to bed. The tendency to communicate across time zones means that just as you're going to bed someone else with an urgent message for you has just arrived at their office and is logging on. Voice mails pile up, creating a moral burden to reply. Mobile phones are everywhere, in restaurants, on trains, in theatres, in cars. The compulsion to answer the mobile always implies that the incoming call is necessarily more exciting, exotic and life affirming than the face-to-face conversation you were having.

I don't know many people who are working less hard than they were ten years ago. Most are working faster with more to do and to shorter deadlines. I was speaking recently to someone in a major oil company who said that the wind-down to Christmas used to begin in mid December and the recovery might run on to the middle of January. Now people are fixing meetings in Christmas week and the whole operation speeds back in to action in the first week of the New Year. As a senior executive put it to me recently, 'Standards of living are much higher now than when I started out, but the quality of life is lower.' Meanwhile many other people have no work at all. This is a different proposition and we'll come back to it shortly.

Progress is a rarely linear. And yet we are all taught to think in a linear way from earliest days to the end of university education. This is why creative people often find themselves at odds with education and why many people who succeed in education find themselves in increasing difficulties. These problems are deep enough to reconsider some of the fundamental assumptions on which we are now basing our systems of education and training.

Academic inflation

When I left university in the 1970s I took it for granted that I would get a job. I just didn't feel like one at the time. Like most of my generation I thought I might head for the Silk Road, sample Tibet for a year or two and map out the further reaches of consciousness. When the time felt right I'd take a look at the job market and see what appealed. I didn't get further than London as it happened, but the principle was the same. Having a degree virtually guaranteed a job and it didn't much matter what the degree was in. It could be in Old Norse, and it often was. Graduates could leave university with a degree in Old Norse and employers would snap them up. 'You can speak the Viking,' they'd say, 'come and run our factory. Your mind is honed to a fine edge.' Just having a degree was evidence of advanced intellectual capacities and of employability. This is not true any more. In most cases having a degree is no guarantee of work at all. It's still much better to have a degree than not, but now it's just a starting point. One reason is that so many people now have them.

The overqualified

As the demand for intellectual labour has grown, the numbers of places in higher education has been increased. In the 1950s and 60s about one in 20 young people in the UK went to university and these came predominantly from the grammar schools. In the current expansion of education, the UK target for entry to higher education is one in three. This is due to rise to one in two. Suddenly, not a fifth but at least half of young people are capable of university level education. What happened in the last 30 years to account for this remarkable change in intellectual capacity? Is it the fluoride in the water; organic farming? The fact is that large numbers of young people have always been capable of higher academic study. Until recently they just weren't needed. But the increasing numbers of graduates bring new problems.

Two-thirds of British universities were established after 1960. From the beginnings of state education, the expansion of the grammar schools went hand in hand with founding of new universities in the major industrial centres.[15] The demand for this began to accelerate rapidly from the 1960s onwards because of the bulge in the birth rate after the end of World War II. Between 1954 and 1966, the numbers of school leavers qualifying for university entrance rose from 24,000 to 66,000. In the 1960s a fleet of new universities was established to meet the demands of these baby boomers. The expansion in higher education in Britain mirrors the massive growth in higher education in America in the 1960s. Some American universities such as Indiana, Madison Wisconsin and Ohio State are the size of small towns. They're turning out highly-qualified students in tens of thousands.

According to the Institute of Employment Studies in the UK, in the last 20 years there has been a doubling of the numbers of graduates on the job market. They have not been matched so far by a similar rise in the numbers of graduate jobs. The numbers of vacancies for graduates dropped by 35 per cent in the recession of the early 1990s. The numbers began to recover as the decade ended especially among large companies. But, in the UK at least, the gap was still considerable. There were graduate opportunities for about 20,000 people, and about 200,000 graduates a year competing for them. Many graduates end up looking for jobs for which they are overqualified. In the 1980s around 30% of all graduates were in non-graduate jobs, at least early in their careers. It is likely that the levels of over-qualification are even higher now. According to the Institute of Employment Studies, we are offering school leavers signposts for the future that were made in the 1960s. We should be creating new signposts for 2020.

A falling currency

There are many reasons for gaining academic qualifications. Taking academic courses should be inherently interesting and rewarding, and the best are. But there is another reason. We assume that qualifications will put us in a better position to find work. Academic qualifications are a form of currency. They have an exchange rate in the market place, for jobs or for more education. But, like all currencies, their value is related to market conditions and can go up or down. We are living now in a period of spiralling academic inflation and it has profound significance for the whole enterprise of education and training. In the 1960s and 1970s a university degree had high market value. This was partly because relatively few people had them and the currency of degrees was high: when many have them the currency tumbles. Then something more is needed to edge ahead of the crowd. Increasingly that is a Master's degree. What happens when that market is saturated and that currency begins to inflate? The signs are there already. For most university jobs, for example, even a Master's degree is no longer enough.

I was a member of a university appointment panel recently for a standard lecturer's post. I asked the chairman of the panel what we were looking for in the candidates. He said, 'I think we are looking for someone with a good PhD'. 'As opposed to what?' I said, 'A dreadful one?' I know what he meant. There was a time when if you had a PhD you were in an élite group – less than one per cent of the population. PhDs were a rare species popularly thought to be kept in separate rooms and to be fed on plasma. There has been a huge growth in PhD students in the last ten years and quality varies. He meant we should look for someone with a PhD from a good university. But, when PhDs have a varying currency rate, where does this spiral end? Nobel Prizes? Do we eventually have Nobel Laureates applying for jobs in primary schools: 'OK, you've got a Nobel Prize but can you play the piano? We need someone for assembly.'

Under pressure

We are putting increasingly high pressure on young people to achieve academic success. This pressure begins in schools when they are five, and continues as they are graded throughout their school careers. The introduction of compulsory tests at key stages throughout primary and secondary education, combined with public examinations for school leaving and university entrance, means that children learn to judge themselves by their grades. Adults today had a light assessment load at school compared with children at school now. By the time they are 16, pupils today will have taken at least three major national curriculum tests. In the UK further compulsory tests will be introduced for four-year-olds from 2003. Clearly, standard assessment tests can provide important information about children's progress and comparative achievement. But there are indications that more and more children are finding the pressure of testing difficult to bear and are suffering from the consequences.

> 'The deaths of four students at one of the country's top universities have highlighted the dangerously high expectations we now have for our children's academic success.'
>
> The Times, *10 May 2000*

For students of 20 or 30 years ago it was almost compulsory to go to university to enjoy yourself, to discover your inner being, to write poetry and to be politically extreme. Your degree result was almost immaterial. Now leading employers demand a 2:1 at least and 'students find there is little time for anything so indulgent as fun or self-discovery'.[16]

> 'Life opportunities are more closely related to degree results than ever before. Coupled with that, children are being examined more than ever before. This loses sight of exams being an indicator of how you are progressing and becomes rather like continually pulling up a plant to see how well it is growing.'[17]

In addition to academic pressure, students are surrounded by a sophisticated lifestyle of high fashion and cappuccino bars in which 'a stylistic error can mean social extinction'. In *Understanding Suicidal Behaviour*,[18] psychiatrist Dr Rory O'Connor of Strathclyde University calls for schools to spend much more time on basic communication and problem-solving skills that children will need to cope later in life:

'There has been a huge change in expectations of young people over the past ten years. More and more are going into higher education and the entry standards at the top have risen. The problem is that this encourages a perfectionist tendency and encourages individuals to put unrealistic pressure on themselves. Some will drink or take drugs or just bottle things up. Our young people need communication and problem solving skills taught at schools from a young age.'

This would help them to tackle the precursors to problems that might lead them to consider suicide: 'Only by getting young people to talk can we tackle the stigma associated with being unable to deal with stress and the reluctance to go to see anyone about it.' Ken Lloyd Jones of the National Union of Students in Scotland says that the main pressure is, paradoxically, to appear as laid-back as possible. 'People are under pressure to be rounded, happy, successful, talented, bright young things and they want to fit in,' he says. 'They are under pressure not to appear under pressure'.

> 'We are not equipping our young people with the skills required to deal with modern life and the increased pressures of continual assessment and being examined at every level. We have always had some form of assessment but the emphasis has shifted. By assuming that academic success is the be-all and end-all of life, we are not teaching people how to deal with the fact that they may not reach the aspiration. We don't teach people how to deal with failure and this is a fundamental oversight.'
>
> *Rory O'Connor*

Academic deficiency

Employers are complaining that academic programmes from schools to universities simply don't teach what people now need to know and be able to do. They want people who can think intuitively, who are imaginative and innovative, who can communicate well, work in teams and are flexible, adaptable and self-confident. The traditional academic curriculum is simply not designed to produce such people. The current assumption is that, by expanding education and raising standards, all will be well. The end game I suppose is that when everyone has a PhD, there'll be a return to full employment. But there won't. The market will reconfigure as the currency rates fall. Employers will simply look for something else. They are doing this already. In these circumstances, employers aim for exactly the same élite they would have taken on 20 years earlier: they just raise the bar and develop different techniques for selecting the people they want and add new criteria.

Degrees have their origins in the times when universities were small, select centres of learning to which only a minority of people were admitted. A degree focused on study in a discipline, its content and methods. Teaching revolved around lectures, small tutorials and seminars. The various personal qualities associated with a degree, independence of mind, objectivity, capacity for abstract thought and reasoned debate grew out of the style and atmosphere of teaching as much as from absorption in the subject. A degree was not seen originally as a direct vocational qualification so much as a general mark of academic achievement. But it was a distinction and as such a genuine advantage in professional careers. We now have mass systems of higher education, which are multipurpose. The opportunities for individual teaching and learning and for a broad liberal education simply do not exist to the same extent. The expectation now is for vocational relevance. The talk is of transferable skills but these don't come as a matter of course. The irony is that the pressure to develop these personal qualities is coming at a time when staff are least able to attend to them because of growing student numbers.

The underqualified

The problems are serious enough for the highly qualified. They are deadly for the unqualified. The relentless drive to raise certain types of academic standard may help those who are driven to achieve them. But it compounds the problems of those who, for whatever reason, are not. There are currently 15 million people unemployed in Europe. Nearly a third of these are under 25. They are part of the widening group of the socially excluded: those who feel marginalised by the driving forces of social and economic change and who are alienated by them or powerless to become involved. Many countries are facing a smouldering problem of social exclusion, as more and more people are left out of work and have little prospect of finding it. The problems are compounded by the

Education and training in Britain 2000

- 31 per cent of all British workers had not been offered formal training by their current employer.
- 5.7 million British adults of working age have no qualifications at all.
- 26 per cent of adults have done no learning in the past three years and 22 per cent of those have done no learning in the ten years since leaving school.
- 20 per cent of all adults in England – around 7 million people – have serious problems with basic literacy and numeracy.[19]

ways in which these groups tend to be concentrated in particular areas: lessening their shared chances of recovery. In Britain, the vast majority of the unemployed live on 2000 housing estates. In a work-driven society, being without work or the prospect of it can produce a deadly result: not always passive submission; it can be an explosive and aggressive counter-attack.

In Chicago and some other urban centres in the United States the problems of gang[20] violence are growing, particularly among the alienated and disaffected. In some areas of Chicago, 30% of young blacks are dead by the age of 21. The greatest need in these gangs is for recognition, identity and respect: the kind that for others can come from work. The same is true of major European cities where, during the 1990s, gang warfare and violence became an increasing feature of teenage life. What will raising traditional academic standards do for people with no hope of work but with the same need as everyone else for hope and recognition?

In 1996, a symposium on *American Creativity at Risk* took place in the United States.[21] It considered some bizarre and troubling statistics. One was the rise in the prison population and its costs compared with investment in education. Prisons, once at the bottom of state and local budgets, have in the past 10–20 years steadily risen towards the top of the budgetary priority list, so that in at least one state, spending for prisons exceeds spending for public education. As one speaker grimly concluded, 'The punitive outweighs the affirmative; the pathological in our society is now more costly to support than the developmental.'[22] In the state of New Hampshire the arts budget has decreased every year though the State budgets have gone up. Fifteen years ago there were 400 people in Concord, the state prison. There are now 2500.

'As troubling as the decline of public [i.e. non-private] school education may be, perhaps even more troubling is the emergence of the socio-political construct known as the permanent underclass. If indeed certain groups of inner-city residents, i.e. Black and Latino, economically disenfranchised, are caught in an irrevocable cycle of crime, poverty and despair, if there is no opportunity for creative self invention, why waste money on developmental institutions like public schools and libraries on those populations. Or so some politicians would want is to believe. Upward mobility, a staple of American life is under assault and with it the possibility of creative reinvention of the individual, also a fundamental aspect of the American imagination.'

Mary Schmidt Campbell

As the symposium concluded, 'if this comparison shocks us, it should also spur us into action because it reflects a change in the nation's priorities away from building the future and toward short-term solutions for the complex social and cultural problems we face.'

In the United States, as in many countries, there is a worrying trend in disaffection and aggression among young people in schools. In the United Kingdom, four out of ten Birmingham secondary school teachers who responded to a questionnaire said that they had suffered physical and verbal abuse in the classroom, nearly two-thirds of them at least once a year. One in 11 teachers said they had been threatened by a pupil with a weapon. Teenage boys between the ages of 14 and 15 are the main perpetrators. Two-thirds of the abused teachers were women. This problem is not unique to Birmingham. If similar surveys were carried out in other parts of the country, it is possible that the same sort of results would be produced. The sense of frustration and demoralisation is strong, with 60 per cent of teachers saying they wanted to leave the school they work in. Half of the teachers surveyed said they wanted to leave the profession because of the poor level of discipline in schools.[23]

'I was dismissing a class for lunch. They were all standing up behind their chairs and just about to leave. I was standing in front of a door with a glass window. A 15- or 16-year-old boy entered the room and wanted to put his bag down before lunch. I told him to wait until the class was out of the room. He was bigger and stronger than me. He pushed me out of the way and put his bag beside a desk; he was arrogant and rude to me. I wanted to have a word with him and asked him to stay behind after the class had left. He pushed me back and I hit the door and banged against the handle. I was lucky not to have gone through the glass. The boy was put in isolation for the day and his parents were involved. They didn't seem that bothered as he lied over what had happened and they chose to believe him rather than me.'

'I was in the corridor and saw a group of four girls make a mess in a classroom by throwing paper and rubbish around. I naturally asked them to tidy up their mess. They refused and were rude and arrogant, saying that I had no right to tell them what to do. They then deliberately pushed past me as a group and knocked me off my balance. I fell against the stairwell and injured my shoulder. I passed on the information to more senior management but, as far as I know, nothing happened to the girls.'

Conclusion

The dynamic interaction of technological and economic change has two immediate long-term implications for labour markets. First, it puts a premium on the capacity of companies, countries and of individuals for creativity and innovation. The most important resources of all companies are now the ideas and creative capacities of the workforce. This is why there is such a huge expansion of education. The second key quality is the need for flexibility and adaptability. International companies, especially those using ICT, will position their operations wherever the best qualified and most cost-effective labour force happens to be. European call centres for example are as likely to be in Delhi as in Paris. The competition for jobs is no longer local or even regional, but global. All of this is but a fraction of the larger cultural equation, which we all have to balance to live our lives effectively.

There are major problems facing all organisations in recruiting and retaining people with creative abilities, powers of communication and adaptability. Yet young people have these in abundance. By the time they emerge from formal education, many of them do not. Clearly there are many complex factors at work. But among them, the existing pressures and nature of traditional academic education are playing a major part. Despite the growing skills gap, the war for talent and the extraordinary pace of change on every front, many policymakers and others continue to chant the mantra about the need to raise academic standards. In doing so they confuse academic with educational and qualifications with abilities. There is an urgent need to rethink some of the underlying assumptions if we are seriously to tackle the development of creative resources in all our people. This is not just a matter of technical change: it means confronting deep-seated assumptions that underpin our view of ourselves and of each other, and the ways in which these are promoted through sustained years of formal education and training. This is a problem of ideology.

Let me say why. There is an important difference between theory and ideology. We may avoid one but it is hard to escape the other. Theory is conscious: ideology is often unrecognised. If you have a theory you know you have it and you can say what it is. Theorising is a conscious and deliberate attempt at explanation. I don't mean just grand theory about the cosmos or the meaning of life: it may be a theory about why your favourite team is doing badly. Ideology is something else. By ideology I mean the fundamental underlying attitudes on which our theories are based: like why you support the team in the first place. I mean the assumptions, values and beliefs that constitute our taken-for-granted views of reality, our natural conception of the way things are. We are all guided in our everyday lives by ideas, values and beliefs that we simply take for granted. They become so much part of our way of seeing things – our worldview – that we come to think of them simply as common sense. These are the ideologies on which we build our theories. The dominant ideologies of education are now defeating their most urgent purpose: to develop people who can cope with and contribute to the breathless rate of change in the 21st century – people who are flexible, creative and have found their talents.

Chapter Two

THE SEPTIC FOCUS

'We pass through this world but once. Few tragedies can be more extensive than the stunting of life, few injustices deeper than the denial of an opportunity to strive or even to hope, by a limit imposed from without but falsely identified as lying within.'

Stephen Jay Gould

Introduction

In this chapter I make four arguments that have a vital bearing on the whole idea of creativity and human resources.

- For historical reasons, education is preoccupied with academic ability. This is based on deep-seated assumptions in Western culture about intelligence.
- Academic ability promotes particular forms of intellectual activity. They are important, but they are very far from being the whole of human intelligence.
- The results have been beneficial in many areas and disastrous in many others. There is a tragic narrowing of intelligence, divisions between arts and sciences, and a profound waste of creative capacity. Very many people leave education never realising their real intellectual capacities.
- In the new world economies, this waste of human resources is potentially disastrous. The abilities that are now most needed are being left to waste despite the massive expansion of education and the pressure

to raise standards. Organisations and communities everywhere are paying the price.

Thinking about intelligence

How intelligent are you? This is not an easy question. There is no agreement whatever among the many different specialists in psychology, neurology, education or other professional fields on what intelligence actually is. And they spend a good deal of their time and intelligence thinking about it. In a detailed account of the idea of intelligence,[24] Ken Richardson describes one survey in the United States in which a large number of psychologists were asked to say what they thought intelligence to be. There was very little overlap in their responses. Of the 25 attributes mentioned, only three were mentioned by 25 per cent or more of respondents. More than a third of the attributes were mentioned by less than 10 per cent of respondents. As Richardson says, 'if we were asking experts to describe edible field mushrooms so we could distinguish them from the poisonous kind and the experts responded like this, we might consider it prudent to avoid the subject altogether.'

Intelligence is one of those qualities that we all think we can recognise in people but the moment we try to define it, it melts from our grasp. There may be no agreed definition but there is a general conception of intelligence that's obvious in public policy on education and in our general culture. It is based on two ideas. The first is IQ (intelligence quotient); the second is academic ability. I think most people assume that the higher a person's IQ, the more intelligent he or she is; and that the more academic qualifications people have the brighter they are. This view is reflected in powerful popular images of intelligence in the media and in daily life. It is profoundly mistaken.

Images of intelligence

For more than 20 years, one of the best-known programmes on British television was a quiz show called *Mastermind*. Each week four contestants took it in turn to sit under a spotlight in a darkened studio. They faced an earnest interrogation by the quizmaster, Magnus Magnusson. There were two rounds: one on a specialist topic chosen by the contestant, and a second on general knowledge. Each week the winner went forward to the later rounds until the Mastermind of the Year emerged from an all-winners final. He or she achieved national celebrity as one of the cleverest people in Britain. *Mastermind* was a television version of a longer-running radio programme called *Brain of Britain*. This had a similar format and each year the ultimate *Brain of Britain* was also tagged as a person of exceptional intelligence. What counts as high intelligence in these contests? What were the winners so good at? In both cases, it is a prodigious memory for information. Many quiz programmes appeal to the same abilities. In the phenomenally successful *Who Wants to be a Millionaire?*, contestants can win a fortune by answering 15 factual questions. Programmes like these illustrate a powerful popular view of intelligence and one that is promoted strongly by formal education. It is that intelligence is a capacity for remembering and recalling factual information including names, dates, events and so on. But take a different example.

Mensa is an international association that sees itself as one of the most exclusive clubs in the world. It claims to admit only two per cent of the population to its membership based entirely on an assessment of their 'high intelligence'. This judgement is based on the ability of applicants to complete various 'intelligence tests' such as the following:

Question 1: What letter should come next?

M Y V S E H M S J R S N U S N E P ?

Question 2: Details of a check at a stationer are shown below.

78 – Pencils
152 – Paint Brushes
51 – Files
142 – Felt Tip Pens
? – Writing Pads

How many writing pads should there be?

What do these tests test for?[25] Mostly, they are looking for an ability to analyse a sequence of ideas and to work out the principles on which the next step is based. Other tests look for related abilities such as visualising the rotations of objects in space.

Question 3: In which direction should the missing arrow point?

```
V  >  ∧  V  <
V  <  >  V  >
∧  >  ?  >  V
>  <  V  ∧  >
V  >  <  V  ∧
```

In their different ways, *Mastermind* and Mensa draw on two important features of intelligence. The first is the capacity for remembering and recalling information. Philosophers call this propositional knowledge. This is knowledge *that* something is the case: for example that the Constitution of the United States was established in 1789; or that the moon is 239,000 miles from Earth. A second feature of intelligence, illustrated by the Mensa tests, is skill in particular types of logical analysis – in working out the principles underlying a sequence of ideas and how the sequence progresses. Often these are examples of what philosophers call logico-deductive reasoning. This is what many IQ tests look for. But what does this really tell us about a person's overall intelligence? What exactly is IQ and how does it relate to academic ability?

Measuring your mind?

Like the Coca-Cola bottle, the petrol engine and the hydrogen bomb, IQ is one of the most compelling inventions of the modern world. It's really an idea in four parts. The first is that each of us is born with a fixed intellectual capacity or quotient: that in the same way as we have brown eyes or red hair, we have a set amount of intelligence. Second, the amount of our intelligence can be calculated by a short series of pencil-and-paper tests of the sort illustrated above. This might take about an hour. The results can be compared against a general scale and given as a number from 0 to 200. That number is your IQ. On this scale, average intelligence is between 80 and 100; above average is between 100 and 120 and anything above 130 puts you among the geniuses and gets you into Mensa's Christmas party. The third proposition is that IQ tests can be used to predict children's performance at school in later life. For this reason, IQ test are widely used for school selection and for educational planning. Finally, IQ is taken to be an index of general intelligence: that is, these tests are assumed to point to a person's overall intellectual capacities. For all these reasons, since the idea of IQ emerged about 100 years ago it has had explosive consequences for education, social policy and for practical politics.

Sir Francis Galton was the cousin of Charles Darwin. After reading *The Origin of Species* in 1859, he became convinced that heredity played a decisive role in human development and that it would be possible to improve the human race through selective breeding procedures. Galton believed that all differences in individual ability reflected differences in genetic inheritance. He turned his attention to developing scientific ways of measuring natural human ability or intelligence. The early intelligence test emerged from his determination to isolate the power of 'general intelligence' and to develop a scientific way of measuring and comparing it between individuals.

Against this background, the modern intelligence test builds on the work of Alfred Binet. At the beginning of the 20th century, Binet was working with children in elementary schools in Paris. He began to develop tests for children of different ages that could be administered easily using short test items. By 1905 he had produced his first scale of intelligence based on a test of 30 items designed for children aged from 3 to 12 years. Binet's intention was to identify children in the Paris school system who might need special educational support. His aim was practical and his method 'was pragmatic rather than scientific'.[26]

Within a few years translations were appearing in many parts of the world: 'The circularity of the strategy and the very restricted context of its uses were soon forgotten in the wake of the social uses to which the test was soon being deployed especially in the United States.'[27]

For generations, IQ has been the basis of selection for different styles and levels of education. It has been used to support and to attack theories of racial and ethnic difference. Early IQ tests in the UK and the USA suggested that poor people and their children have low IQs and that the rich and their offspring have high IQs. It seemed that IQ somehow determined levels of affluence and of material success. These findings provided a powerful rationale for political initiatives to improve the human stock by selective breeding and population control, a policy known as *eugenics*. This had been one of the founding interests of Sir Francis

'In using the Binet test, the tester simply worked through the items with each child until the child could do no more. Performance was then compared with the average for the age group to which the child belonged. If a child could pass the test expected of a six-year-old, say, the child was said to have a mental age of six. Binet used the difference between the mental age and the chronological age as an index of retardation. In 1912 German psychologist William Stern proposed using the ratio of mental age to chronological age to yield the now familiar intelligence quotient or

$$IQ = \frac{mental\ age}{chronological\ age} \times 100$$

'Thus was born first modern intelligence test.'

Ken Richardson

Galton. In the early 20th century, leading intellectuals including Winston Churchill and George Bernard Shaw supported the eugenics movement, arguing that the breeding of the poor should be carefully controlled. Some states in the USA legislated to sterilise people classified as 'idiots' or of low intelligence. With different motives, the Third Reich embraced eugenics as a key element in the Final Solution.

A major controversy about IQ flared up in 1992 with the publication in America of *The Bell Curve* by Charles Murray and Richard Hernstein.[28] *The Bell Curve* argued that IQ tests do point reliably to vast differences in human intelligence. It argued that IQ is linked to low moral behaviour and that there is a connection with the cultures of some ethnic groups especially black and Hispanic communities. *The Bell Curve* was widely condemned as a racist tract and has generated an inferno of debate, which is still raging. From the outset, IQ has been a powerful and provocative idea, and it remains so despite the fact that there is no general agreement on exactly what IQ tests measure, nor on how whatever it is they do measure relates to general intelligence.

The tip of the iceberg?

Few of us would doubt that the capacities for propositional knowledge and for logico-deductive reasoning are important features of intelligence, that they are types of intellectual ability. The problem we face is implicit in Mensa's view of itself as the organisation of high intelligence, and in the very titles of *Mastermind* and *Brain of Britain*. It is the extent to which these particular types of intellectual ability are now confused with intelligence as a whole: that is, the extent to which they are seen as intelligence rather than as aspects of it. The most important example of this is education itself. Formal education is obsessed with these abilities. They underpin success in schools, colleges and universities and they are what the most influential systems of examination look for and reward.

Think back to your own time in education. For generations, children and students have spent most of their time writing essays, doing comprehension exercises, taking tests of factual information, and learning mathematics: on activities that involve propositional knowledge and forms of logico-deductive reasoning. Some lessons promote other sorts of ability. Most schools have art lessons and some music, perhaps playing an instrument or being in a choir; and sport. Some subjects, including technology, have a practical element. But practical subjects are typically at the margins of formal education. The main forms of assessment are still written examinations that test factual knowledge and critical analysis. This pattern continues into higher education, and especially in universities: for most people the highest form of higher education.

Some years ago, I was a member of a university promotions committee, a group of about 20 professors from the arts, sciences and social studies. A university lecturer is expected to do three kinds of work, teaching, administration and research. A case for promotion has to include evidence of an acceptable standard in all three. One of my roles as head of my own department was to make recommendations to the committee about promotion. I'd recommended an English lecturer who I thought was a sure case. The committee required members to leave the room when their own recommendations were being discussed. I thought this was a routine case so I slipped out of the room and was back in a few minutes ready to rejoin the meeting. I was kept waiting for nearly half an hour: clearly there was an issue. Eventually I was called back into the room and sat down quietly. The vice-chancellor said, 'We've had a few problems with this one. We're going to hold him back for a year', meaning that they were not approving his promotion. Members of the committee are not meant to question decisions that concern their own recommendations, but I was taken aback. I asked why, and was told there was a problem with his research. I wasn't prepared for this, and asked what was wrong with it. I was told there was so little of it.

Well, this was an English lecturer. In the period under review he'd published three novels, two of which had won national literary awards; he'd written two television series both of which had been broadcast nationally and one of which had won a national award. He had also published two papers in conventional research journals on 19th century popular fiction. 'But there is all of this', I said, pointing to the novels and the plays. 'We're sure it's very interesting', said one of the committee, 'but it's his research we're worried about', pointing to the journal papers. 'But this is his research too', I said, pointing to the novels and plays. This lead to a good bit of shuffling of papers. By research, most universities mean papers in academic journals or scholarly books. The idea that novels and plays could count as research clearly hadn't entered the debate. But a good deal hangs on this. The issue was not whether these novels or these plays were any good, but whether novels and plays as such could count as research in the first place. The common sense reaction was that they could not. But what is research?

In universities, research is defined as a systematic enquiry for new knowledge. So I asked the committee if they thought that novels and plays could not be a source of new knowledge. If so, does the same apply to music, to art and to poetry? Are we really saying that knowledge is only to be found in research journals and in academic papers? This question is vitally important, for a number of reasons. It relates particularly to the state of the arts and sciences in universities and in education more generally. There's an intriguing difference in research in arts and science departments in universities. If you work in a physics or chemistry department, the research you do is physics or chemistry. You work in a laboratory and you do science. You don't spend your professional life analysing the lives and times of physicists. If you are a mathematician you do mathematics. You don't scrutinise the mood swings of Archimedes or his relationships with his in-laws when he developed his theories. Scientists do science. But this is not what goes on in most arts departments.

Professors of English are not employed to produce literature: they are employed to write about it. They spend much of their time analysing the lives and drives of writers and the work they produce. They may write poetry in their own time: but they're not normally thanked for doing it in university time. They're expected to produce analytical papers about poetry. Producing works of art often doesn't count as appropriate intellectual work in an arts department: yet the equivalent in a science department, doing physics or chemistry does. So why is it that in universities writing about novels is thought to be a higher intellectual calling than writing novels; or rather if writing novels is not thought to be intellectually valid why is writing about them? What's going on here? I think the answer lies in academic illusion.

The groves of Academeia

Politicians and others tend to think of all education as academic, and to describe all children as either academic or non-academic. But whatever general intelligence may be, academic ability is not the same thing. Academic ability is very specific. It is based on the two capacities for propositional knowledge and for logico-deductive reason. This is what 'academic' means. The term derives from the name of a grove near ancient Athens called *Academeia*. It was there that, 400 years before the birth of Christ, the Greek philosopher Plato established a deeply influential community of scholars. Plato's teachings drew from the methods of philosophical analysis that had been developed by his teacher, Socrates. Plato's own student, Aristotle, developed these further in his own work and teachings, and from them have grown systems of thought, of mathematics and of science that have helped to shape the intellectual character of the Western world.

The benefits have been enormous and so have the deficits. I'll come back to these later. But the immediate point is that the priorities of education throughout the West are now dominated by the idea of academic ability and by the related idea of IQ. Both offer a disastrously limited picture of human intelligence and both result in a lethal waste of human resources in education, business and in the community at large. The clear and present danger is that both of these ideas have assumed the status of ideologies, of taken-for-granted ideas about the way things are. How has this happened? How did the idea of IQ come to be so powerful? How does it relate to the idea of academic ability and how have these two ideas come to dominate our conceptions of education, intelligence, and so often of ourselves? The answer lies in the triumph of science in the last 400 years and in its roots in the groves of Academeia.

The triumph of science

In the Middle Ages it was taken for granted that the sun orbited round the earth. There were two reasons for this belief. First it obviously did. The sun came up in the morning, passed through the sky and went down again at night – much as it does now. It was obvious to everyone that the sun was moving and not the earth. People weren't being flung off the planet on the way to work: there wasn't a network of ropes to hang to on the way to the shops. It was obvious that the sun was moving and we were not. This was a common sense view based on everyday experience. But there was a religious reason too. In the medieval worldview, the earth was the centre of creation and human beings were God's last word, the jewel in the cosmic crown. From a theological perspective, the earth had to be at the centre of the universe with all the other heavenly bodies moving around it. Theologians also assumed a perfect symmetry in the universe. The planets, it was thought, revolved around the earth in perfect circular orbits.

Poets including Shakespeare expressed this harmony in the rhythms of verse; and astronomers based elaborate theories upon it. Mathematicians from the early Greeks developed elegant formulae to describe these motions. The problem was that there were worrying variations in these movements. The planets wouldn't behave. Assuming that the earth was the centre of things, the mathematicians worked out increasingly intricate variations in their theories to account for these variations. As perplexed as everyone else, Copernicus and Galileo made a radical new proposal. What if the sun wasn't going round the earth: what if the earth was going round the sun? This startling idea solved at a stroke many of the old problems that had plagued astronomers. Later, Kepler showed that the planets didn't move in circles but in elliptical orbits. This was later explained by the effects of gravitational attraction. Their reward for all this was persecution and in some cases execution. For the Churches, Galileo's proposal amounted to heresy, an affront to God's design and to humanity's view of itself. Copernicus, Galileo and Kepler did not solve an old problem: they changed the whole basis on which the old questions had been asked. The old theories were shown to be wrong because the basis on which they had been built was mistaken.

Historians conventionally think of Western history in three main periods – ancient, medieval and modern. The Renaissance marks the shift from the medieval to the modern worldview. It saw the most extraordinary flowering of intellectual achievement on all fronts. In little more than 150 years, some of humanity's greatest figures were born and some of our greatest works produced: lives and achievements that have shaped the world that we now live in. Between 1450 and 1600 Europe saw the birth of Leonardo da Vinci, Michelangelo, Raphael, Galileo, Copernicus, Shakespeare and Isaac Newton. They produced works in art and literature of unsurpassed beauty and depth, and created the foundations of modern science, technology and philosophy. The Renaissance was so called because it marked a rebirth of interest and discovery of classical learning: of the insights and methods of the ancient world, of Greek philosophy, literature and mathematics. The Renaissance marked a determined break with the medieval worldview, a break that was made possible by a succession of technical innovations and accomplishments. Four in particular were to prove decisive: the printing press, the mechanical clock, the magnetic compass and the telescope.

The invention of the printing press unleashed a philosophical and social revolution. Before print, only a small, literate élite had access to books, ideas and learning, an élite largely confined to the Church. Printing books created an unprecedented democracy of ideas. This unleashed a process that resulted in the need for widespread literacy. This in turn challenged the authority of the literate over the illiterate. The hold of the Church was based on its exclusive access to scriptures. Printing fuelled the growth of public debate on social values and politics, and led in short to the widespread diffusion of ideas and thought on a scale previously unimaginable. Through books, ideas could be disseminated and absorbed across national and cultural boundaries

'The invention of printing by Gutenberg, but most importantly the development of the portable book by Aldus Manutius (1450–1515) of Venice, created the personal library and revolutionised for ever the control of knowledge. For the first time, the institution of the medieval library and the institutions behind it began to be undermined, most notably the Church, with its combination of creation and repository of knowledge. The medieval institution started to be replaced by a commercial product: the independently published portable book. A new technological and intellectual transition started, which reinforced the conditions of the scientific revolution and accompanied the great period of the discoveries. The portable book had a subversive impact, created the conditions for the Reformation, for the use of vernacular language, for the diversification of publishing and allowed for a great individual expression of authors and readers. It also created the instruments for the development of bureaucracy and large organised states. It greatly expanded the community of knowledge. Publishing became the vehicle for the transmission of ideas and debate, for proselytism and for scholarly recognition. The seeds for the Enlightenment were sown and with them the belief in education and, in this century, the belief in universal education and literacy.'

Dr Juan F. Rada

The mechanical clock made possible new ways of thinking about time and freed people from the natural rhythms of day and night in their working lives. This proved hugely important in generating new patterns of work. The magnetic compass made possible new ways of exploring the earth's surface, and led to a new and more precise knowledge of the continents. The telescope made possible more accurate and specific observation of the movements of the planets and of the place of the earth in the heavens.

As Toffler notes, the clock came along before the Newtonian image of the world as a great clock-like mechanism, a philosophical idea that has had the utmost impact on our intellectual development. Implied in this image of the cosmos as a great clock were ideas about cause and effect and about the importance of external as against internal stimuli that now shape our everyday behaviour. The clock also affected our conception of time so that the idea that a day is divided into 24 equal segments of 60 minutes has become almost literally a part of us.

Through the complex and interwoven changes of the Renaissance two key themes emerged. The first was a new emphasis on the importance of individual experience. The second was a new faith in the power of reason as the true source of knowledge.

The rise of the individual

Each major period of intellectual growth and development has been characterised by key ideas that have driven forward the sensibilities of the times. The Enlightenment was driven forward by the ideas of rationality and of evidence. In the medieval period Church and State were locked in a close embrace. Before the invention of printing, only clerics had access to the scriptures and the word of God. This gave them unrivalled control over the people's minds. The Renaissance and the great cultural movements that flowed from it gradually shook loose the iron grip of the Church. The shift from Ptolemy's view of the universe with the earth at its centre to the universe of Copernicus was shattering. It was a fundamental and dramatic change from a view of the world that was based on the evidence of the senses to one based on the argument of reason and interpretation. The arguments of Copernicus and Galileo raised serious doubts about some aspects of religious teaching, though they both denied being atheists. The intellectual adventure they began led in the 19th century to Darwin's theory of evolution. This was an intellectual earthquake that shook the whole structure of religious belief.

As literacy spread, the flow of ideas increased and the supremacy of the Church declined. This process was accelerated by the growing unrest in the 15th century with the spiritual and political corruption of the Catholic Church. In the early 15th century the German cleric Martin Luther sparked a revolt against the perceived corruption of Rome: a movement that spread throughout Europe and split Christianity in two. The Reformation put a new emphasis on the individual's direct relationship with the creator and on the individual understanding of the scriptures. The emphasis on the knowledge and understanding of the individual underpins the growth of science and the scientific method in the 16th and 17th centuries. As the old certainties of the Church fragmented, philosophers and intellectuals began to ask fundamental questions about the nature of things. Specifically, what is knowledge and how do we know. In answering these questions they developed the intellectual methods and techniques of the ancient Greeks that have been rediscovered in the Renaissance.

I think, therefore I am

The view of the Enlightenment was that the medieval worldview had relied too much on uncritical sensory data and on religious dogma. The philosophers and scientists of the Enlightenment began by trying to take nothing for granted. The French philosopher Descartes began by assuming that nothing should be taken on trust. If a new edifice of knowledge was to be constructed, it must be built brick by brick with each element fully tested. Descartes asked what, if you want to understand the world, is the minimum we can take for granted, given that everything around is suspect. He began to try to set out a logical programme of analysis of experience where nothing else would be taken for granted that could not be proved either logically or through experiment and empirical data. He came to the conclusion that the only thing he could know for certain was that he was thinking about the problems. This is the one thing he could not doubt, therefore his fundamental starting point was his *cogito ergo sum*, 'I think, therefore I am'. I must be alive because I am thinking.

The idea of a Renaissance Man is of one who is learned in a range of disciplines including the arts and sciences. In our own times a quintessential Renaissance figure is Leonardo da Vinci, a man gifted in painting, sculpture, mathematics and science. When Michelangelo was painting the Sistine Chapel he had in his room drafts of scientific theorems and of new technological innovations. This union of the arts and sciences gradually dissolved in the 16th and 17th centuries. The driving forces of the Enlightenment and of the modern worldview have been rationalism and empiricism. The aim has been to see the material world as it is stripped of superstition, myth and fantasy. Knowledge has to meet one or both of two tests: to conform to the strict dictates of deductive logic or be supported by the evidence of observation. This period saw spectacular achievements in science and technology, achievements that led directly to the Industrial Revolution of the 18th and 19th centuries and to the dominance of science in all its forms in our own times.

Rattling the cage

The medieval theories were built on a false ideology. The Renaissance was a change of paradigm: a shift not just in theories but in the fundamental basis of thought, a change of ideology. The term *paradigm* is overused and often wrongly applied. It was popularised in 1972 by the American philosopher of science, Thomas Kuhn.[29] He used it to refer to the great epochal changes in human thought and culture that have characterised scientific change and progress. A paradigm is an accepted framework of rules, assumptions and points of view that define established ways of doing things. A paradigm is not a single theory or scientific discovery, but the approach to science itself within which theories are framed and by which discoveries are verified.

A paradigm change is a process in which one tradition is replaced by another. Kuhn describes science as a puzzle-solving activity in which problems are tackled using procedures and rules that are agreed within the community of scientists. Kuhn was interested in the moments in history when there is a shift either in the problems or in the rules of science or both. He sees a difference between periods of 'normal science', when there is a general agreement among scientists about the problems and the rules, and periods of scientific revolution. These are when, for a variety of reasons, an established paradigm is replaced in whole or part by a new one.

These revolutions typically happen when normal science begins to generate results that the accepted rules and assumptions cannot account for. This is exactly what happened in the late medieval period. If these anomalies persist and accumulate there can be a loss of confidence in the accepted methods and a professional crisis in science. This crisis can unleash periods of great creativity and invention, periods of extraordinary science. These periods create opportunities for completely new theories about the nature and limit of science itself and these theories can generate completely new questions and rules. The Renaissance of the 14th and 15th centuries was such a period. Eventually the revolution subsides and a new paradigm emerges. For a time it provides the framework for a new and different period of normal science. During the Renaissance the old medieval worldview was shaken and eventually replaced by a new one: a new intellectual age.

What's the question?

The intellectual horizons of a society or of an historical period are not set simply by events or human desires. They are set by the basic ideas that people use to analyse and describe their lives. Theories develop in response to questions. And a question, as Susan Langer notes, can only be answered in a certain number of ways. For this reason the most important characteristic of an intellectual age is the questions it asks – the problems it identifies. It is this rather than the answers it provides that reveals its underlying view of the world. In any intellectual age there will be some fundamental assumptions that advocates of all the different ways of thinking unconsciously take for granted. These deep-seated attitudes constitute our ideology and they set the boundaries of theory by inclining us to this or that set of issues and explanations. If our explanations are theoretical, our questions are ideological.

Revolutionary ideas can transform our understanding in many different areas. As Susan Langer puts it: a new idea is a light that illuminates things that simply had no form for us before the light fell on them and gave them meaning. We turn the light here, there and everywhere the limits of thought recede before it.'[30] The transition from the medieval to the modern world was a genuine paradigm change. The insights of Copernicus and Galileo came at the dawn of a new way of seeing the world. They repositioned not only the earth in space but humanity in history. It was not just a shift in astronomy, but a whole new vision in philosophy, religion and politics.

The new paradigm was based on the ideas of logical reasoning and of evidence. These were revolutionary and generative ideas. A generative idea is one that creates massive excitement in many different fields because it opens up whole new forms of explanation, new ways of seeing and thinking. These powerful ideas of reason and evidence took hold of the intellectual world of the 15th and 16th centuries. Slowly at first and then with increasing speed they challenged the accepted scientific theories, religious beliefs, superstition and myth that had helped to shape the medieval worldview. In Europe in the 17th and 18th centuries, the period now known as the Enlightenment, these ideas ran with irresistible force through science, philosophy and politics, bowling over traditional methods of thought and opening up vast new fields of adventure in science, the arts and philosophy. The extraordinary advances in technology that resulted from the new sciences led directly to the social earthquake of the industrial revolution in the 19th and 20th centuries.

Our present worldview has been hugely shaped by the rapid scientific, technological and cultural revolutions that emerged from this paradigm shift from the medieval to the modern world. In the process, the explanatory powers of logic and of scientific evidence, and the intellectual authority of science as a whole have become firmly implanted in our own worldview. They are part of modern ideology and they interact powerfully with how we think and create theories in every field. Education is a prime example. The dominant systems of education planning and organisation in the 20th century were moulded by the economic assumptions of the industrial worldview. The values and priorities of education were shaped by attitudes to intelligence that have evolved within the dominant paradigms of scientific understanding. They have shaped our basic understanding of ourselves, of our own capabilities and of who we are.

The rise of education

From 1944 the British education system was provided through two types of schools, grammar and secondary modern. The grammar schools were much more prestigious. Other European countries had similar systems. Grammar schools have deep roots in British and European history. But what are grammar schools? Why are they so called and why are they so prestigious? Nowadays, a grammar school means a selective secondary school that provides an academic curriculum for young people aged 11–18. These are distinguished in England from secondary modern schools by the nature of the curriculum and from comprehensive schools by the fact of selection. In the United Kingdom, grammar schools are popularly thought to represent the highest forms of secondary education. How did they achieve this position?[31]

Grammar schools of various sorts can be traced back to the ancient Greeks. The term *grammar school* first appeared in English in 1387 in the form *gramer scole* but its Latin form *schola grammatica* was in use at least 200 years before that. The Kings School Canterbury claims to be the oldest grammar school in England. It traces its origins to the coming of St Augustine in AD 597. The institutions themselves may have originated more than 1000 years earlier. Originally a grammar school was literally one that taught grammar and especially Latin grammar. Grammar with its alternative form gramarye and glomerye was highly revered by the uneducated who regarded it as a form of magic, a meaning that survives in our modern word 'glamour'.

In the Middle Ages in Europe, education was largely provided by the Church. Many of the earliest grammar schools were founded by religious bodies. Some were attached to the larger or collegiate parish churches; others were maintained by monasteries. The purpose of these grammar schools was to educate boys for the Church, but medieval clerics followed careers in many fields. The Church was not one profession but the gateway to all professions including law, the civil service, diplomacy, politics and medicine. The main subjects of study in the ancient and medieval schools were linguistic and literary. The principal focus was on learning Greek and Latin literature and the aim was to be fluent enough in these to enter professional life in law, politics or the civil service.

Latin was the international language of the Church and fluency in it was a vital accomplishment. Given their specialist functions, grammar schools have always been selective. From earliest times, they saw themselves offering a specialist form of education that would benefit some and not others. On this basis they have long provided some form of selective entrance test. By end of the 15th century there were 300 or more grammar schools in England and the Church was involved in most of them. As the 15th and 16th centuries unfolded and produced a deepening scepticism of religious doctrine, many non-religious organisations began to establish their own schools for their own purposes. Many of these were related to trade.[32] The growing influence of grammar schools of all sorts was accompanied by gradual changes in what they actually taught.

In England the term public school, *schola publica*, appeared in the 12th century. The term distinguished them from private or home-based schools. It meant that they were open for those who could afford to send their children to them: literally public in that sense. The idea of superiority of public schools developed in the 19th century when a group of specific schools emerged that was catering specifically for fee-paying aristocrats and middle-class parents. In the Victorian period a clear class division had begun to emerge in the grammar school system and two types of school began to evolve. There were the denominational boarding schools, typified by Rugby, which catered for the sons of the rich and ruling classes. And there were the day schools in the towns catering for the less affluent but aspiring middle classes. The so-called public schools emerged from both groups, but especially from the boarding schools. Essentially public schools are a particularly prestigious and self-appointed group of independent grammar schools.

The grammar-school curriculum

The curriculum of the medieval grammar schools was deliberately narrow and at first it was specifically classical. For centuries, the domination of the classics on the very idea of being educated resisted many attempts at reform. Some pioneering head teachers tried to loosen the grip of the classics on the grammar-school curriculum by introducing other subjects and a more practical approach to teaching them. Richard Mulcaster, the first headmaster of the Merchant Tailors' School from 1561 and 1586, tried hard to have English taught at grammar schools, arguing that it was essential to regulate its grammar and spelling. He pressed the case for drama in schools and his boys performed before Elizabeth I on a number of occasions.

> Classical education was based on the seven liberal arts or sciences:
>
> - grammar – formal structures of language;
> - rhetoric – composition and presentation of argument;
> - dialectic – formal logic;
> - arithmetic;
> - geometry;
> - music;
> - astronomy.
>
> The first three were known as the *trivium* and formed the basis of the grammar-school curriculum. The remaining four, the *quadrivium*, were the foundation of the university curriculum.

The curriculum of Merchant Tailors' School came to include music and drama, dancing, drawing and sport of all sorts – wrestling, fencing shooting, handball and football. Francis Bacon argued for the inclusion of other subjects, including history and modern language, in the school curriculum. Above all he argued for science to be taught in schools. The headmaster of Tonbridge School published a book in 1787 arguing for the curriculum to include history, geography, mathematics, French, and artistic and physical training. Charles Darwin went to school at Shrewsbury. Reflecting on the experience, he said:

'Nothing could have been worse for my mind than this school as
it was strictly classical, nothing else being taught except a little
ancient geography and history. The school as a means of education
was to me a complete blank. During my whole life I have been sin-
gularly incapable of mastering any language ... The sole pleasure
I ever received from such (classical) studies was from some of the
odes from Horace which I admired greatly.'[33]

Darwin was ridiculed by his headmaster for his strong interest in chemistry. His friends nicknamed him 'Gas'.

Little progress was made in these attempts to broaden the curriculum
beyond the classics until the mid-19th century. The pressure for change
eventually came from elsewhere. Three developments in particular were
to reshape public opinion about schooling and to reform the grammar-
school curriculum. The first was the growing impact of science and technology, and the changing intellectual climate of which they were part.
Second, the rampant growth of industrialism was changing the whole
international economic landscape. The Exhibitions of 1851 and 1862 viv-
idly illustrated the rapid industrial progress of other European countries, a process that had begun in Britain but was now threatening to
outrun it. Third, new theories were developing about the nature of intelligence and learning. The new science of psychology was proposing new
explanations about intelligence and how it should be cultivated. These
challenged accepted assumptions about how children learned, and the
benefits of a strictly classical education rooted in learning grammar and
formal logic.

Educating everybody

In 1870 the government passed an Act of Parliament to develop provision for primary schools. In 1902 the government addressed the provision of secondary education and began to establish county grammar
schools. By 1908 there were 663 grammar schools and by 1963 there were
1295. This massive expansion was directly related to the development
of the industrial economy and the need for a better-educated worked
force.[34] The 1944 Education Act provided free secondary education for
all. This was an enormous social advance and opened new routes to millions who had been denied them. From the outset, the grammar schools

had been seen as a means of social advancement and as superior to the secondary moderns. One of their main purposes was to provide a route to the universities. Parents expected that children qualifying for grammar schools would be in a good position to go on to university, take a degree and have a life of secure professional employment. It was in this context of rapid social change and educational expansion that the idea of IQ took such a firm hold on the public mind.

Sheep and goats

Selection for the different types of school was by a national test taken at the age of eleven, the *eleven-plus*. Less than a quarter of children were accepted for a grammar school education. The rest, having failed the eleven-plus, went to secondary modern schools. Understandably many thought of themselves as educational failures. They include people in business, in education, in the arts, sciences, and in many other walks of life. They may have been spectacularly successful in their own fields, they still carry a belief that they're not as clever as they make out, because they failed the eleven-plus. In my experience many people who took the eleven-plus thought of it like a blood test. If you have a blood test it tells you a biological fact about yourself: for example, whether your blood is Group O or A. And there is no point in complaining about the result. Your blood group is what it is. Many people think of the eleven-plus and similar tests in the same way: that they tell us something equally factual, in this case, whether we are clever or not. It's as if a litmus paper was dipped into your brain. If it changed colour, you were clever: if it didn't, you weren't. Some of the most successful people I know still carry the burden of failure at eleven.

The interaction of educational theory and scientific ideology is illustrated by the controversy over selection at eleven-plus. The principle of selection was to distribute children to schools according to their different abilities and attitudes. It depended in practice on finding reliable ways of identifying for each child what those abilities and attitudes were. This is what the eleven-plus was designed to do. It was based on scientific theories about intelligence (IQ) and its measurement, a system known as psychometrics. The critics argued that the tests took no account of the influences of social background and educational opportunity on young people. It was also clear that the tests were very limited. In apparently testing abilities across the full range, they actually monitored only a narrow strip. High scores relied to a large extent on standard verbal and logical operations. Despite their now obvious shortcomings, challenging the authority of these tests was not an easy matter.

They had the powerful backing of government and of significant parts of the scientific establishment. They gained their elevated status because for a considerable time it was taken for granted that they must be 'above reproach or beyond social influence, conceived in the rarefied atmosphere of purely scientific inquiry by some process of immaculate conception'.[35] But the critics weren't just concerned with the technicalities of the tests but with the whole idea of IQ and of psychometrics. They attacked the basic assumption that science could measure the abilities and potential of people in the same way as it could measure rainfall or high tides. Changing attitudes to intelligence-testing was not just a matter of pointing out theoretical inconsistencies. The criticisms were not theoretical: they were ideological. There are two myths about the eleven-plus. Each of them has a more general significance.

The top 20 per cent?

The first myth is that only 20 per cent of children were capable of passing the test. This was not true. Only 20 per cent of children were required to pass it. The numbers of grammar school places were planned on that basis. It was harder to pass the eleven-plus in some parts of the country than others because of local variations in the numbers of grammar schools.

> An official survey in 1962 showed that in Bootle in Liverpool 12 per cent of thirteen-year-olds went to grammar school; in Merthyr Tydfil in Wales the figure was 40 per cent. In Pembrokeshire, a boy or girl whose IQ was around 115 was probably safe for a grammar school place. In Putney he or she would have had a reasonably good chance, 'but just four miles away at the other end of the boat race at Mortlake would have been a poor bet'.[36]

It was harder in some years to pass the eleven-plus. If there was a particularly good year and 30 per cent or more performed well, the authorities didn't build more grammar schools or requisition old army camps to cope with the surplus. They raised the pass level.[37] It was generally harder for girls to pass. Girls tend to mature earlier than boys and often perform better at such tests and not so many girls were expected to go into professional and managerial jobs. The prospects of passing the eleven-plus were greatly increased by coaching. Success relied as much on knowing the techniques involved as on natural aptitude. Taking these tests unprepared is like taking a driving test without learning to drive. Someone who hasn't been taught might say 'I can't drive', and they'd be right. They're not incapable of driving, they just don't know how. If they said they couldn't fly they'd be right in a more literal sense. Many who failed the eleven-plus might have passed with training and many of those who did pass had had it. When children failed the eleven-plus they weren't told it was for economic reasons. They assumed they just weren't as clever as those who passed. There was much talk of 'parity of esteem' meaning that all children were valued equally. But this was hard to credit when those who passed went to the prestigious grammar schools and the 'failures' went to the secondary moderns. The whole point of the eleven-plus was to find grammar school material – the 'top 20 per cent'.

Academicism

The second myth about the eleven-plus was that it was a test of general intelligence. It wasn't. It was a test for the particular abilities that were promoted in the grammar schools: that is for academic ability. One of the great problems that face the future of education is the persistent confusion of academic ability with intelligence. The word *academic* is commonly used as a synonym for *educational*. Politicians say we must raise standards in schools. When asked which standards they're likely to say academic standards. So are most people. The idea of academic ability is so much part of our thinking about educational achievement that this just seems like plain common sense. This is where the difficulty lies. The conflation of academic ability with intelligence is simply taken for granted. It is in this sense an ideology. Like many ideologies, this one persists despite all evidence to the contrary.

This is not a party-political issue. Politicians of all persuasions are curiously united in this respect. They argue over the funding and organisation of education, over access and selection and about the best ways to improve standards. But it is rare to hear politicians of any party raise questions about the absolute importance of academic standards. Politicians tend to be focused on short-term objectives and electoral advantage. They see few votes in arguing against the dominant conceptions of academic excellence or in opposing the mantra of 'back to basics'. There is a powerful tendency to play to the received wisdom on these issues. In any case, most politicians claim no special expertise in education beyond their own experience of it and the assumptions of common sense. Like many others they argue that the standards that applied to them at school should apply to everyone else now and in the future. They do this whether or not their own experiences at school were good or bad, successful or otherwise.

Academic ability is not the same as intelligence. Academic ability is essentially a capacity for certain sorts of verbal and mathematical reasoning. These are very important, but they are not the whole of human intelligence by a long way. If there were no more to human intelligence than academic ability, most of human culture would not have happened. There would be no practical science or technology, no business, no arts, no music, no dance, drama, architecture, design, cuisine, aesthetics, feelings, relationships, emotions, or love. I think these are large factors to leave out of an account of intelligence. If all you had was academic ability, you wouldn't have been able to get out of bed this morning. In fact there wouldn't have been a bed to get out of. No one could have made one. You could have written about the possibility of one, but not have constructed it. Don't mistake me, I think that academic work – and the disciplines and abilities it can promote – are absolutely vital in education, and to the full development of human intelligence and capacity. But they are not the whole of them. Yet our education systems are completely preoccupied with these abilities to the virtual exclusion of many others that are equally vital – capacities that becoming more important every day.

Assessing the legacy

Our present systems of education have been moulded by these assumptions of industrialism and academicism. These may have been justified for their times. The social and personal cost to generations of people has nonetheless been considerable. The system divided families, as brothers and sisters were sent in different directions, and it broke up communities and friendships. It stamped impressionable children with an indelible view of themselves as clever or not: a self-image that has persisted throughout the lives of millions of people. Some politicians may think it has been a price worth paying. But it is not justified now.

In some respects the benefits of the rationalist scientific worldview have been incalculable. They include:

- the extraordinary advances in medicine and pharmaceuticals and their impact on the length and quality of human life;
- the explosive growth in industrial technologies;
- sophisticated systems of communication and travel; and
- an unprecedented understanding of the physical universe.

There is clearly much more to come as the catalogue of achievements in science and technology continues to accumulate. But there has been a heavy price too, not least in education. There are three major deficits:

- the division of the arts and sciences;
- the division of intellect and emotions; and
- the narrowing of intelligence.

Arts and sciences

During the 20th century the classics became almost extinct in secondary education. In their place is a new tyranny. The school curriculum of the late 20th and early 21st centuries has settled into a familiar pattern. At the centre is a dominating concern with literacy, numeracy, with mathematics, science and technology. The arts and humanities are typically on the periphery. The Enlightenment led to a powerful reaction in the late 18th and early 19th century, the reaction of Romanticism. Where the Enlightenment was represented by the great rationalist philosophers and scientists, Hume, Locke, Descartes, Romanticism was carried forward in the powerful works of artists, poets and musicians, especially Beethoven, Schiller, Byron and Goethe. The Romantics were focused on the quality of human experience and on the nature of existence. The divisions of the Enlightenment and Romanticism are alive and well in contemporary attitudes to the arts and sciences. Typically the sciences are associated with fact and truth. The image of the scientist is a white-coated boffin moving through cold calculations to an objective understanding of the way the world works. In contrast, the arts are associated with feelings, imagination and self-expression. The artist is pictured as a free spirit giving vent to a turmoil of creative ideas. In education the impact of these assumptions has been far reaching. The sciences enjoy high status: the arts suffer from low status. Many young people have to choose between them at 14 or 15, and then head down different corridors. In most Western systems of education the arts are on the periphery, the sciences at the centre. There are three reasons for this.

The narrowing of intelligence

Doing the arts as distinct from writing about them is not part of the rationalist view of intelligence. Making music, painting pictures, involvement with drama, and writing poetry are not associated with academic ability. The clearest evidence of this view is in the universities, as illustrated by my battle for the promotion of the English lecturer. Universities are devoted to propositional knowledge and to logico-deductive reasoning. University scholars can look at anything – plants, books, weather systems, particles, chemical reactions or poems – through the frame of academic enquiry. It is the mode of work that distinguishes academic work, not the subject matter. The assumed superiority of academic intelligence is obvious in the traditional structure of qualifications. Traditionally universities have rewarded academic achievement with degrees. Other institutions give diplomas or other sub-degree qualifications.

If you wanted to do art, to paint, draw or make sculptures, you went to an art college and received a diploma for your efforts. If you wanted a degree in art, you had to go to university and study the history of art. You didn't do art at university; you wrote about it. Similarly if you wanted to play music and be a musician you went to a conservatoire and took a diploma: if you wanted a music degree you went to a university and wrote about music. These distinctions are beginning to break down. Arts colleges do now offer degrees and university arts departments are beginning to offer practical courses. But there is still resistance to the idea that degrees should be given for practical work in the arts. This is because universities in particular and education in general are still dominated by the ideology of academicism.

Work and leisure

The arts are not thought to be relevant to employment, but science and technology are. The arts are valued for recreation and cultural development, but they are not thought to be useful in a practical way. During the industrial period there was an element of truth in the employment argument. But in the new economies there is not.

> While programme budgets for education, art and basic science research have continued to shrink, Americans have been drawn to these fields in unprecedented numbers. The number of people who now call themselves artists has exploded from 400,000 in 1950 to 1.7 million in 1990 according to the American Assembly's statistics. There are 3.2 million Americans (2.7 per cent of all US workers) working for cultural organisations, and there has been an enormous increase in the past decade in the numbers of orchestras, opera companies and theatres. Despite this dramatic growth, the federal government has slashed spending on the arts. The 1996 budget for the national endowment of the arts of $99.5 million represented a 39 per cent reduction from the previous year.[38]

The biggest growth areas in the developed economies rely precisely on the qualities the arts promote. In any case, the idea of linear routes from education to work never was wholly sound and it's less so now than ever before. A related reason is that, unlike the sciences, the arts are strongly associated with the idea of talent. It is taken for granted that everyone has some capacity for mathematics and everyone has to do it. But the arts are associated more with the idea of special ability, with gifts and talents than with routine capacities. If people seem to have particular abilities they may be encouraged, but often not otherwise.

Favouring the few

The academic curriculum values two abilities above all others: a particular sort of critical analysis and short-term memory. The most common form of assessment in schools and universities is still the timed written examination. Success requires a good short-term memory: the ability to retain factual information at least until the examination is over. Some people need to work hard for months to achieve this and develop elaborate systems to stimulate their memory during the exam. Others can do the same work in a few weeks or days. As the currency of academic qualification inflates, the pressure to achieve higher results is increasing with often catastrophic consequences. In 1770, Lord Eldon gained his Oxford degree with a relative lack of effort. He was asked two questions: 'what is the Hebrew for the place of the skull?' and 'who founded University College?' In 2001 university students are sacrificing everything to get ahead of the pack. These are the pressures for those with strong academic interests. But what about the others whose real interests or abilities lie elsewhere? For them education has always been an alienating experience. The sense of alienation is compounded by the structures of schooling; the subject divisions, the 40-minute periods, the bells and the queues.

Another brick in the wall

The septic focus is a specific example of a deeper assumption in the Western worldview, the idea of linearity. The rationalist moves through a logical sequence, building one idea on another like bricks in a wall. The empirical method similarly looks for patterns in events, suggesting movements from known causes to known effects. A great deal has happened in the theory and practice of science and philosophy to question these sequences. Chaos theory and complexity theory for example both try to grapple with the apparently chaotic relationships between events. But education continues to be planned on the assumptions of a linear progression from cause to effect.

There is a problem in the UK in levels of literacy. As a result, a special literacy programme has been introduced to all schools. Sensible enough, you might say. But to make way for it, the rest of the primary-school curriculum was 'relaxed' for two years, including the arts and humanities. The assumption was that the best way to improve literacy was to focus on it to the exclusion of everything else. The domination of science and technology in the school curriculum is also based on the assumption that the economy needs more scientists. The assumption is that science should be compulsory in all schools so that all children will understand science and many more will become scientists when they grow up. In practice this is not necessarily what happens. After ten years of a compulsory core curriculum in science in the UK there is no evidence at all that there has been a net increase in the number of students taking science courses in universities. Nor has there been an improvement in the quality of science-teaching or in the public understanding of science. The academic worldview assumes that the correlation must exist, so planning proceeds as if it does, despite all the evidence to the contrary.

There is a natural and accepted view that one of the main purposes of education is to prepare young people directly for a place in the labour market. Obviously, general education should do this. But there are two complications. First, thinking of education as a preparation for something that happens later can overlook the fact that the first 16 or 18 years of a person's life are not a rehearsal. Young people are living their lives now. What they become and what they do later depends on the attitudes and abilities they develop as they are growing up. Linear assumptions about supply and demand can and do cut off many potentially valuable and formative experiences on the grounds of utility. The focus on apparently useful subjects is a vivid example in education of *the septic focus*. It's what leads schools to think that some subjects are more important than others.

Second is the fact is that we can't predict any more what the economy and labour market will look like 5 years from now – let alone 10 or 20. All that we do know is that it is changing at a phenomenal rate and in radical ways. In any case, for most people there never has been a direct, linear progression from education to a planned career. Our lives are too buffeted by the currents and cross-currents of social forces and personal impulse. For most people, life after school is shaped by an unpredictable mixture of events and opportunities. They make sense of it only retrospectively when writing a curriculum vitae. Then the basic human urge for narrative takes over, to make a chaotic process of randomness and chance read like a well crafted scientific trajectory through life.

Most geography graduates for example don't follow careers that are directly relevant to their degrees. A wide range of jobs is opening up to geographers led by marketing, financial services, accountancy and social work. In 1996 a quarter of geography graduates stayed on in higher education for further study and training. Most of the remaining three-quarters went into employment. The most common destinations included accountancy, banking and management consultancy. Geography is the fourth largest supplier to the financial services sector. Martin Frost from King's College, London, has analysed recent changes in the labour market for geography graduates. He notes that the key drivers of change are the decline in manufacturing jobs, the rapid increase in jobs concerned with selling and training, and the high premium now placed on technological literacy, creativity and imagination and the increasingly youthful and mobile character of the workforce. The proportion of those under 30 in these 'new' jobs was almost double that in the 30-plus age group.[39]

Rock music is another example of the non-linearity of real life. The great surge in rock music in Britain in the 1960s and 70s owed little if anything to music education in schools or colleges. For example, Paul McCartney was actually refused a place in his school choir because he was not thought to be very musical. Some of the most notable figures in rock music at that period attended higher education. But they did not go to music schools. They went to art colleges. The pedagogic traditions in art schools provided an atmosphere of experimentation, personal creativity and hip culture that were totally lacking in the formal conservatoire atmospheres of the music schools. In all these respects the art colleges provide an unexpected breeding ground for rock culture.

Beyond the ivory tower

The domination of academicism is curious. It is assumed to be essential for personal success and national competitiveness. Yet the whole idea of academic work is also thought to be separate from the real world. Calling any argument academic is a put-down implying it is out of touch with reality. Academics are thought to live in ivory towers and to know little about the lives that real people lead. In any case, university education was always perceived more as a preparation for the professions, the law, civil service, medicine and education than for business and trade. In Britain for many years, going into business was frowned on in polite circles. This has been changing over the past generation. Successive governments have taken initiatives to broaden the range of qualifications and to develop work-experience schemes. Partnership programmes have been encouraged between education and industry including placement in companies for headteachers.

'The arrival of the knowledge economy has intensified the competitive pressures on higher education. Learning has become big business. A new national initiative is needed to maximise Britain's chances of success in this global environment. We want to create a new partnership between universities and the private sector which will develop a novel means of distance learning and exploit the new information and communication technologies. It will concentrate resources from a number of partners on a scale which can compete with leading US providers. If we are to become a leading knowledge-based economy, we must create new routes into higher education and new forms of provision. Our historic skills deficit lies in people with intermediate skills, including highly qualified technicians. We have to develop new higher education opportunities at this level, orientated strongly to the employability skills, specialist knowledge and broad understanding needed in the new economy. Universities need to adapt rapidly to the top-down influences of globalisation and the new technologies as well as the bottom-up imperatives of selling the local labour market, innovating with local companies and providing professional development courses that stimulate economic and intellectual growth.'[40]

Universities have seen the opportunity for new programmes. Most leading universities now have business schools that pursue business-related research and offer various Master's programmes for business people. These programmes meet several needs: the need for business people to extend their own education, and enhance career prospects through studies that are directly related to the work they do. They also meet the need for universities to expand their own activities and bank balances.

But there are consistent and resistant problems beneath the surface. Despite all the attempts to promote parity between academic and vocational courses, the attitude persists that academic programmes are more demanding and offer higher status. As Peter Scott[41] puts it, the university system has become a mass system in structure but remains élite in its private instincts. In universities, business schools are valued for their contribution to the balance sheet but have relatively low academic status. Philosophy and mathematics departments may generate little income but their intellectual capital is very much higher. In some ways these are typical problems for new disciplines.

All new fields of study tend to be disparaged by established subjects. In the 17th century, science itself had to fight for respectability in education. In the 19th century psychology was treated with contempt by many serious scientists. So too was sociology in the 1960s. A similar problem exists with cultural studies now. It is seen as a hybrid field with no serious intellectual core of its own. Business schools are beginning to be treated with intellectual respect as well as financial gratitude. But for some universities this may be too late.

> 'University education as traditionally conceived has been undermined sociologically by increasing social diversity and professionally by the collapsing belief in objective knowledge and scientific truth.'
>
> *Peter Scott*

The corporate university

Universities are lumbering institutions and change tends to take place at a glacial rate. Businesses need better training now. Rather than wait for universities to catch up, some have raced ahead in their own way. Many are now offering not only their own training programmes, which they have done for years. They're also establishing their own in-house universities and awarding their own degrees. In 1981, Motorola was the first company in the United States to develop a corporate university (CU). Today there are hundreds of such initiatives throughout the world. A recent report, *The Future of Corporate Learning*,[42] drew from case studies of 12 such initiatives. All were designed to meet the learning needs of their businesses in imaginative ways. A corporate university is defined as:

> 'An internal structure designed to improve individual and business performance by ensuring that the learning and knowledge of a corporation is directly connected to its business strategy. A corporate university's students are drawn from its employees. It has the capacity to offer formal accreditation for some of the learning it provides.'[20]

The best CUs are about more than simply integrating provision to cut costs. The principal purpose is to develop learning opportunities that reflect each company's strategic business goals. Jean Meister surveyed CUs in the United States, and identified three themes that were common to the curricula for employee development:

- inculcating corporate citizenship;
- giving all employees understanding of the business's contextual framework; and
- developing specific workplace competencies that define the business's competitive advantage.

I recently spoke at a national conference for the Marriott group of hotels and was followed by the award of degrees to the first Marriott graduates. One of them said to me that this was her first real experience of educational success. She had done very well in the company and in her commercial life generally even though she'd failed at school. This was the first time she'd been on an education programme that uncovered her real strengths and raised her self-esteem and confidence as a learner.

> The Lloyds TSB group is the UK's largest financial services company and employs 76,000 people worldwide. Launched in July 1999, its university is integral to the group's overall business plan and has two main objectives:
>
> - making learning more accessible to staff; and
> - ensuring a closer link between the learning available and the needs of the business.

The involvement of senior company executives and directors as faculty heads helps ensure this focus. The learning itself is offered through a number of approaches including online. Participation is voluntary but does form part of the performance development process for those involved. It reflects a group-wide trend towards workplace learning, with employees having access to the facilities through:

- a centralised personnel and training call centre to provide advice on training and career opportunities;
- a Website available on both the Internet and the corporate intranet;
- 2000 multimedia PCs accessible to all staff members;
- learning cybercafés at major group premises;
- 30 regional training centres and three residential training sites for face-to-face courses; and
- the facility to order learning materials such as books and videos for delivery to the workplace.

Facing the future

The present rate and scale of technological change means that we are facing a paradigm shift in the ways in which we live and earn our livings. It needs to be met by a comparable paradigm change in how we think of education. We need to rethink some of the fundamental ideas that we have come to take for granted as simple common sense: about education, intelligence and ourselves. For years academic education has taken precedence over everything else for economic and vocational reasons. Now that these assumptions are crumbling, it is time for a more fundamental revision of our expectations about what education is for, and of what it should do to meet the extraordinary tide of changes that are engulfing us all. We need a new ideology, a new paradigm, not just a new theory. To construct it we need to take stock of the real human resources we have with which to face them. We need to revisit the economic and intellectual assumptions on which we educate our children and on which we have based our view of ourselves and the people around us.

Conclusion

Our ideas can enslave or liberate us. The shift from medievalism to the modern age was a change in ideology, not just in theory. The natural history of a paradigm change is that there is turmoil in the transitional stages. Eventually the new ideas settle into a pattern and in due course they become part of the new, revised worldview – the new ideology. Paradigm changes may be triggered suddenly by events or inventions or insights, but the transition from one intellectual age to another can be traumatic and protracted. Some people never do make the transition and remain resident in the old worldview, their ideological comfort zone. Those who see the future and ride ahead to meet it are often thought of as mad or heretical, or worse. The modern worldview is dominated still by the ideology that came to replace medievalism: the ideology of rationalism, objectivity and of propositional knowledge. These ideas frame our attitudes and theories every bit as much as myth and superstition underpinned the painstaking calculations of the medieval astronomers. Just as their ideology created the framework for their questions, so does ours.

We ask how can we measure intelligence? The underlying assumption is that intelligence is quantifiable and lends itself to numerical measurement. We ask how we can raise academic standards. The unasked questions are the most important of all. What are academic standards, and why do we have such faith in them to deliver the future? Like the medieval astronomer we continue to believe, despite all the evidence that the system is failing us and the people in it. We ask where can we find talented people but we ignore the talents of people that surround us. We look but we do not see, because our common-sense assessment of their abilities distracts us from what's actually there. We ask how to promote creativity and innovation but stifle the processes and conditions that are most likely to bring it about.

The world economies are caught up in a genuine paradigm change. The new technologies do not mean simply that we have new ways of doing things we did before: businesses, organisations and individuals everywhere are faced with entirely new forms of work, leisure and ways of being. We are trying to meet this new social and economic paradigm using the assumptions and preoccupations of the old intellectual paradigm of education. There are profound consequences for the development of creative abilities and for the whole idea of human resources, education, training and economic competitiveness. Many companies are losing the war for talent because they fail to recognise the talent in their midst. Their perceptions of the abilities of those they employ are too often framed by the educational backgrounds they bring with them and by the roles into which they are placed as a result.

The relationships between education and the world we actually live in are being stretched to breaking point. They need now to be entirely rethought. This process should begin by reframing the abilities we all have, and reassessing the skills and aptitude that are now most needed for personal fulfilment and for economic success. The preoccupation with academic ability is an example of a functional fallacy: the tendency to confuse a particular purpose with a general one. One of the functions of education is to develop academic abilities. This does not mean that the function of education is wholly academic. Education has an economic function: this does not in mean that the functions of education are wholly economic. Education has many social, personal and community purposes that have to be balanced with broader economic functions. Human intelligence includes the capacity for academic activity; this does not mean that academic activity is the whole of intelligence. To educate people for the future, we must see through the academic illusion to their real abilities, and to how these different elements of human capacity enhance rather than detract from each other. But what exactly are these capacities and what should be done to release them?

Chapter Three

KNOWING YOUR MIND

'Is man what he seems to the astronomer, a tiny lump of impure carbon and water impotently crawling on a small and unimportant planet? Or is he what he seems to Hamlet? Or is he both at once?'

Bertrand Russell

Introduction

We are all born with extraordinary natural capacities. How these develop is affected by many factors, including how and if they are actually used. There are three characteristics of human intelligence that have fundamental importance for understanding the nature and processes of creativity:

- intelligence is multifaceted;
- intelligence is interactive and dynamic; and
- each of us has a different profile of intellectual and creative abilities.

To develop creative abilities we need to recognise how rich they are and the conditions under which they will emerge.

All in the mind

Liz Varlow is a viola player with the London Symphony Orchestra. In 1999 she received the prestigious Frink Award. She was born in Birmingham, and started playing the violin at the age of eight. She won two scholarships to the Royal College of Music, and went on to win numerous prizes. She is described by fellow musicians as a very fine musician who has developed her musical sensitivity to the highest levels. What sets her apart is that she is profoundly deaf. Her hearing began to deteriorate at the age of 16. By the time she was 19, she had become profoundly deaf for reasons that have never been established. Nonetheless she has maintained her capabilities as an outstanding professional musician. How does she perform without hearing?

'How does anyone play? I know how to make sounds and also know how what I'm doing sounds. A "normal" hearing player does this too. They make sounds and use hearing to check it. It's too late afterwards if the note is out of tune. With the benefit of a fine aural memory, a solid technique and a good sense of humour I have been able to deal with all professional situations and found deafness to be little handicap.'

The idea that a deaf person can be a virtuoso musician is counterintuitive. How can it be possible to play music without the specific sense that seems most essential to producing it? Ms Varlow's achievement demonstrates some of the extraordinary capacities of the human mind, its flexibility and virtuosity.

The ghost in the machine

How do we think? Or rather what are the physical processes in the brain that are associated with the mental experience of thinking? Philosophers and scientists have argued long and hard about the relationship between the mind and the brain. The ancient world saw only a tenuous link. The functions of the mind that we now associate with the brain were then thought to be located in the heart and the lungs. The brain was thought to be the home of the soul. The brain lives remotely from the rest of the body in a cage of bone. It looks like a crinkled ball of flesh and has no moving parts. To the ancient anatomists it seemed the most likely home for that enduring part of the human being that passed into the afterlife. It had no obvious function otherwise.

By the Middle Ages anatomists had concluded that the brain did play a part in human perception and action. As anatomical studies became more sophisticated, they gradually revealed the physical connections between the brain and the rest of the body through the spinal cord and nervous system. But the debate still continues about the exact relationship between the still grey substance that makes up the material brain, and the thoughts, feelings and desires that constitute the human mind. The fact that there is a relationship between the mind and the brain is easy enough to establish. Removing the brain does bring consciousness to an abrupt end. But exactly how the mind arises from the physical matter of the brain is not yet known. How is it that a ball of flesh smaller than a melon can generate the insights of Isaac Newton, the music of Mozart, the dance of Martha Graham, the poetry of Shakespeare and the spiritual longings of Gandhi? How do we account for what has been called the ghost in the machine?

In the last 30 years there have been spectacular advances in the study of the brain, many of them made possible by the new techniques of brain scanning. This technology tracks the patterns of electrical activity in the brain during different activities. This has made it possible to study the workings of living brains. A number of groundbreaking research programmes throughout the world have shed new light at two levels on how the brain works. There is a growing understanding of the functions of the different regions of the brain and of how they interact. There are also new discoveries at molecular level about the electrical processes of the brain. Both fields of research have implications for how we should think about intelligence and about creativity.

Mapping the mind

All normal human brains are physically similar. They are about the size of a melon and look like a large walnut. The upper side seems to be in two halves and has a series of convoluted folds. This is the cerebral cortex or new brain. It's conventionally thought of as being in four regions or lobes; *parietal, frontal, posterior* and *anterior*. The two hemispheres of the brain are connected by a thick shaft of nerve fibres known as the *corpus callosum*. Underneath the brain and to the back is a smaller cauliflower-shaped area known as the cerebellum or old brain. Coming out of that and connecting in to the spinal cord is the brain stem.

Scholars have long thought that different parts of the brain have different functions. In the ancient world and the Middle Ages it was believed that the mind consisted of different faculties, and that each of these was located in a different part of the brain. These faculties included memory, imagination and logical reasoning. This theory was used as a justification for the classical curriculum of the grammar schools. Memory, it was thought, was trained by learning Latin vocabulary, logical reasoning by geometry, imagination by poetry and music. Perhaps the most sophisticated version of this idea was developed in the 18th century by the Austrian scientist Franz Gall.

He studied the brains of hundreds of dead people and tried to match their shapes with the personalities of their owners. Just as most human brains are similar in appearance, most skulls are the same general shape. On closer inspection they have distinctive bumps and hollows and individual variations in shape and size. From his analyses of brains and skulls, Gall developed an elaborate theory about personality, brain shape and the patterns of bumps on the skull. This technique was known as *phrenology*, literally the 'study of the mind'. Gall identified 32 personality traits all associated with different patterns of bumps on the skull. The phrenologists believed that there was a direct link between specific functions, such as speech, and different regions of the brain. Subsequent research effectively destroyed this idea of separate isolated faculties. The American psychologist Thorndyke showed that learning poetry or Latin vocabulary did not improve the memory in general but merely the skill of learning poetry or Latin vocabulary. Studies into brain-damaged patients in the 19th century showed that the idea of specific locations for particular functions was also false. But 'the idea of centres of memory, emotion and so forth still persist in folklore visions of the brain'.[43]

In the 1950s the American scientist Roger Sperry conducted a series of ingenious experiments that suggested a new approach. They involved people whose brain hemispheres had been separated by cutting the corpus callosum so that they operated independently. Sperry found that the 'split-brain' subjects could perform two completely unrelated tasks simultaneously, for example drawing a picture with one hand while writing with another. He concluded that the two hemispheres of the brain fulfilled different but complementary functions. The left side of the brain was largely involved in logical procedures including language and mathematics; the right hand side of the brain was more concerned with holistic operations such as the recognition of faces and orientation in physical space.

This research provoked wide interest, not least in education. It suggested a physical correspondence in the brain to the two great traditions in Western European culture. The left hemisphere seemed to relate to the logico-deductive analysis of the Enlightenment and the scientific method: the right hemisphere to the Romantic impulses of beauty, intuition and spirituality. Educational reformers were quick to argue that the academic education system was in effect almost wholly left-brained. James Hemmings drew a striking conclusion. Educating people entirely through the left-brain activities of the academic curriculum was, he said, like training somebody for a race by exercising only one leg while leaving the muscles of the other leg to atrophy. Others went too far. I remember reading an article by someone who had half-digested the implications of this research. She said she had written in blank verse because she had only used the right hand side of her brain. This remark suggested that she hadn't used either side. The point is not that the two halves should work separately but together. Carl Sagan captured this exactly. There is no way to tell, he said,

> '… whether the patterns extracted by the right hemisphere are real or imagined without subjecting them to left hemisphere scrutiny. On the other hand, mere critical thinking without creative and intuitive insights, without the search for new patterns is sterile and doomed. To solve complex problems in changing circumstances requires the activity of both cerebral hemispheres. The pattern to the future lies through the corpus callosum.'[44]

Research now shows that the brain lights up in different configurations according to the activity in hand. Different areas of the brain are strongly associated with particular functions but they participate in other processes too. Even in their primary functions they rely on the complementary activities of other areas of the brain. The right frontal lobe is focally responsible for music and if it is damaged, musical abilities are impaired. But this section of the brain can't produce music by itself. It relies on connections with other areas of the brain for its proper functioning. Similarly, the loss of a leg affects the ability to walk, but a leg on its own is not much of a walker at all. Speech is a particularly interesting example of how patterns of brain activity vary. When someone is speaking her native tongue her brain configures in one way: it configures in different ways when speaking a second language learned after infancy. These differences in the gross functions point to important features of how the brain functions at the neural level.

A good deal of the brain's activities is not apparent to the conscious mind. Much of its work is a silent traffic with the rest of the body's automatic functioning: with the involuntary processes of bodily metabolism, glandular functions and the complex perceptions of taste, smell, touch, vision, hearing, and so on. Conscious thought accounts for only a proportion of what the brain is doing at any given moment. But conscious or unconscious, the functioning of the brain is a vastly complex process of electrical impulses across the neural synapses. Learning skills and knowledge are associated with a growing complexity of these neural networks. A newborn baby has immense neural capacities. Again language is a powerful example.

> There is a common-sense distinction between mind and consciousness. In one sense, consciousness is what you lose when you go to sleep and regain when you wake up. It is a state of being awake and aware of your surroundings. But consciousness has a second meaning, that of understanding. It is in this sense that we talk of raising consciousness of an issue. The mind is what is being conscious. Babies are born with a brain. They develop a mind as they grow, absorb and reflect on their experiences.

If children are born into multilingual households, they learn all the languages they are regularly exposed to. Parents don't teach children to speak in the way they're taught languages in school. Mothers don't teach their babies the principles of grammar. They prompt and guide and teach particular words. But learning a language is so complex that teaching it formally to an infant would be impossible. Teaching them three or four languages would be unthinkable. Yet infants do learn three or four languages and more if necessary. They don't reach a point of saturation or ask for their grandmothers to be kept out of the room because they can't handle another dialect. They absorb them all. This is because they have a language instinct. Their capacity for languages means that they absorb all the languages they're exposed to. It isn't that multi-lingual households give birth by good luck to linguistically gifted children. All 'normal' children have this capacity. But if a child is born into a home where only one language is spoken that is the language they learn. Learning a second language in adolsecence is much more difficult.[45] One of the reasons is that by then our latent language capacities are no longer so accessible.

From birth and during infancy the child's brain is tremendously plastic. How the brain develops, the networks that are created, depend on how it is used. If the language capacity is not used it may fade as the brain's neural capacities are turned to other uses. The same can be true of music or mathematics or whatever. Susan Greenfield gives a startling example of this. She tells of a six-year-old Italian boy who was blind in one eye. The cause of his blindness was that at a crucial period in his infancy his eye was covered with a patch. The result of this was that the neural networks, which facilitate sight from that eye, became re-deployed, causing permanent blindness. As children grow, their brains are customised, hard-wired, around the uses they make or do not make of them. This may apply to language, sight, music, whatever.

In the South Pacific many young children are accomplished underwater divers. They develop the abilities to swim underwater for long periods so that they can gather pearls, a vital skill for economic survival both for them and their families. In New York, most children do not have this ability. There are very few skilled pearl divers in the Bronx. There isn't the demand. But it's reasonable to assume that the average New Yorker translated at an early enough age to the South Pacific would learn the necessary skills. Living in the Bronx they may have the capacity but not the need nor, as a result, the ability.

Studies of the brain suggest three crucial themes for understanding creativity:

- the variety of human intelligence;
- the dynamics of human intelligence; and
- the individual nature of intelligence.

The variety of intelligence

The founding perception of modern philosophy is the idea that we all live in two distinct worlds. There is a world that exists whether or not you exist. This is the world of objects, events, other people and material things. This world was in existence before you were, and will continue after you have gone. But there is another world that exists only because you exist. This is the world of your private consciousness, sensations and feelings. This world came into being when you were born and will end when you die. We share the first world with each other: we share the second world with no one. This is the world in which, as the psychologist R.D. Laing put it, there is only one set of footprints.[46] The recognition of the difference between *our* world and *the* world marks an important stage in the development of independence and personal identity. How then do we come to see the external world as we do? At one level, it's because of the way we are built. We live in a rich sensory environment surrounded by sights, sounds, smells, temperature and textures, but we can only perceive some of it.

The field of perception

The nature of our senses determines our field of perception – what we are able to perceive and how. As human beings we are typically between five and six feet tall, we stand upright and our bodies are broadly symmetrical. Unprotected, our bodies can endure only small variations in heat. We have five obvious senses: sight, taste, touch, hearing and smell. Our eyes are at the front of our heads and we have binocular vision. We can see light that has a wavelength from about 400 nanometres (extreme violet) to about 770 nanometres (extreme red). Our ears can normally hear sounds in the range 20–15,000 Hz. Other animals have different, often more specialised senses and they inhabit different sensory worlds. Some mammals such as bats can detect ultrasonic frequencies well above 15,000 Hz. Some animals and birds can detect infrasound or low-frequency sound. Pigeons can detect sounds as low as 0.1 Hz. Elephants communicate using sounds as low as 1 Hz. Consequently, two animals living in the same environment may have entirely different views of what's going on. Compare the lives of a seahorse and a killer whale, living in the same stretch of ocean. They may inhabit the same environment but they live in completely different worlds. One factor is their relative size and strength. But they are also equipped with entirely different sensory capacities.

Your own view of the world would be quite different if your senses were more sensitive: if you could hear the sounds that bats hear; or see the world as cats do; or had the smell receptors of a dog. It would be transformed if you had different senses and abilities: if you could see sounds, or breathe indefinitely underwater or fly. Our physical constitution determines our *field of perception*, what we *can* perceive of the world. There are other factors that affect what we actually do perceive. These are cultural factors and they too have a vital significance for the development of creativity. We'll come back to them in *Chapter Five*.

More than meets the eye

We tend to regard as intelligent those who can organise their thoughts coherently, express them clearly and come to reasoned conclusions. I think this holds as a general perception of intelligence. The problem is that it is often limited to those who are particularly good at reasoning verbally and mathematically. But is this really all there is to intelligence? Doesn't composing music involve intelligence? Certainly playing it does. Think about the knowledge and control that's involved in learning an instrument and in understanding musical forms and expression. And what about playing sports, designing buildings, relating to other people, flying aircraft and so on? Aren't these examples of intelligence? If human intelligence were limited to the abilities measured in IQ tests, most of human activity would stop or would never have started. The fact is that we can think in many other ways too.

We not only perceive the world in vision, we think visually. We not only hear things, we can think in sound. Many of our thoughts occur as visual images. Reflecting on the past and anticipating the future is often a process of visualising them. Visual artists think and communicate in images. They aren't trying to express ideas that would be better put into words. They are having visual ideas. Musicians think in sound. We think about our experiences in all the ways we have available. There have been various attempts at formulating categories to express this idea of ways of thinking. A recent version is by the American psychologist Howard Gardner. He defines intelligence as the ability to solve problems in a given context:

'[Consider] a twelve-year-old Puluwat in Caroline Islands who has been selected by his elders to learn how to become a master sailor. Under the tutelage of master navigators he will learn to combine knowledge of sailing stars and geography so as to find his way around hundreds of islands. Or consider the 14-year-old adolescent in Paris who has learnt how to program a computer and is beginning to compose works of music with the aid of a synthesiser. A moment's reflection reveals that each of these individuals is demonstrating a high level of competence in a challenging field and should by any reasonable definition of the term be viewed as exhibiting intelligent behaviour.'[47]

Gardner argues that we all have 'multiple intelligences'. He argues that there are least seven different types of intelligence. In later work he accepts that there are not simply seven discrete intelligences but others too. I think it is better to avoid formal categorising and to recognise that intelligence is multifaceted. We think visually, aurally, spatially, kinaesthetically and in other ways too. These are not so much forms of intelligence as examples of the inherent complexity and variety of intelligence. Intelligence in these and in many other ways goes well beyond conventional conceptions of verbal and mathematical reasoning.

The dynamics of intelligence

It is Saturday morning in Hong Kong. A specialist programme is being held to accelerate mathematical ability. A group of children sits with a specialist teacher for intensive mathematics lessons. The children, aged between eight and twelve, sit with an abacus on their desks. The teacher calls out calculations for them to do: 1289 multiplied by 15822; 22348 divided by 4019. As soon as he finishes calling the numbers, a forest of arms shoots into the air. Each child has the correct answer. The children use an abacus for their calculations, flicking the beads across the bars at lightning speed. Another boy is asked to use an electronic calculator for comparison. He loses every time. The teacher then asks the children to put the abacus away. The answers come just as quickly. The children have internalised the operation, visualising the abacus in their minds' eyes and seeing the answers. Many forms of mental process, in science and in the arts, are visual. Most schools ignore the visual character of intelligence, and in many other forms too. Recognising the dynamics of intelligence can improve academic achievement, not detract from it.

In even the simplest of actions, many different areas of the brain are used, often simultaneously. There is clearly some localisation of function. This is obvious in the effects of damage to the brain, and through differences in individual development. Brain scanning shows that different regions combine during different mental processes. We experience these dynamics in our own thoughts and actions. Speaking is usually accompanied by a dazzling variety of physical movements, facial expressions and gestures. Dance seems to be quintessentially a physical and kinaesthetic form of intelligence. Choreographers design dances with a passionate attention to visual design and movement in space. They are also responding to the expressive qualities of the music or sounds that relate to the dance. For the audience dance is a visual art. Mathematics may seem to be wholly logical, but mathematicians often think visually too.

Scientists, like artists, often make intensive use of visual imagery, both in formulating their ideas and in explaining and expressing them. In *Insights of Genius: Imagery and Creativity in Science and Art*, Arthur I. Miller describes how artists and scientists alike seek a visual representation of both the visible and invisible worlds. In the Renaissance, there were intimate relations between the arts and sciences. With the appearance of Newtonian science in the late 17th century and the age of rationalism, many educated people considered science to be the only source of absolute truth. Miller argues that this view began to change noticeably by the end of the nineteenth century as both arts and sciences began to move towards greater abstraction.

Perhaps the most extraordinary evidence of the holistic functioning of the brain comes from those who don't have a normal range of sensory abilities. Their achievements are startling even where they seem most disadvantaged. At the beginning of this chapter, I outlined the achievements of Liz Varlow. Evelyn Glennie is one of the world's most accomplished percussionists. In 1995 she was voted Musician of the Year. She travels the world giving virtuoso concerts to huge public acclaim. Her many records and CDs have sold millions and have won a variety of awards from professional music organisations. Evelyn Glennie is in demand worldwide to lead master classes on musicianship, but she became profoundly deaf at the age of twelve as she was beginning to develop her musical abilities. She has persisted in developing these abilities despite the lack of the one sense that most people would consider critical to their fulfilment.

Such examples defy ordinary logic. How can someone who is deaf become an outstanding musician? How can this happen when they evidently lack the specific ability on which musicianship depends, a sense of hearing? Both these cases illustrate among other things the holistic, dynamic operations of human intelligence. Evelyn Glennie experiences the music with her whole being. Playing in bare feet she absorbs the musical patterns, vibrations and rhythms through her body in ways that transcend ordinary concepts of sensory perception. In this sense the mind itself may be likened to an orchestra comprising specialist functions and sections but fulfilling its role by dynamic interaction of these elements in ways that make the whole much greater than the sum of the parts.

The individuality of intelligence

So-called *idiot savants* are people who display extraordinary capacities in some areas of intelligence and below average abilities in others. Thomas Greene Bethune was a blind slave boy given to a Colonel Bethune of Georgia in 1850 at the age of one.[48] He was described by a contemporary, Dr Edward Sequin, as being an 'idiotic musical genius' and, more pointedly, as 'idiotic for any other purpose and can accomplish nothing but gyrations and melodies … Until five or six years old he could not speak, scarce walk and gave no other sign of intelligence than this everlasting thirst for music. But at four years already, if taken from a corner where he laid dejected and seated at the piano, he would play beautiful tunes.' According to contemporary accounts, Tom never attended school but he was incapable of learning in areas other than music.

> 'He was restless and explosive and required constant supervision. He seemed irresistibly drawn to the piano and within a few years without any instruction whatsoever he could listen to a piece of musical once, then sit down at the piano and play it through note for note, accent for accent, without error and without interruption.'[49]

From the initial stirrings of his musical abilities at the age of four until his death in 1908, his talent showed no sign of abating. He began a concert career at the age of seven under the supervision of Colonel Bethune, which flourished and continued until his master's death. His career even included a performance at the age 11 at the White House for President James Buchanan. His dependency upon the Colonel, and subsequent decline into depression and belligerence following the death, caused him to retire from the stage at the age of 53. There are four features of Thomas Bethune which are striking:

- He could play the piano without any instruction and without the ability to read musical notation.
- He could recall immediately and play perfectly by ear alone any composition upon first hearing – one account refers to his recalling and playing immediately two new pieces 13 and 20 pages long respectively.
- Despite a verbal vocabulary of only about 100 words, he could memorise a vast repertoire of music – he is said to have known more than 5000 works by such composers as Bach, Beethoven, Mendelsohn, Chopin, Verdi, and Rossini.
- He did not merely recall or imitate other pieces – he began improvising at the piano at the age of six and much of his own practice time was devoted to his own creations.

Astonishing though the case of Tom Bethune is, his is just one of a large number of cases of musical savantism. Other cases have been recorded of extraordinary visual capacities, of prodigious abilities in memory, or in mathematical calculation. In all of these cases the individual shows extraordinary capacities, well beyond any normal expectations, combined with a generally below average or even sub-normal abilities in other mental operations.[50]

The problem in conventional assumptions of intelligence is that there is a single measure. People are thought to be more or less intelligent on a single scale based on the ideas of IQ and academic ability. The conventional question to ask of someone's intelligence is, 'How intelligent are they?' A more accurate question may be, 'How are they intelligent?' There are four related points to emphasise.

- *We all have many forms of intellectual capacity and abilities, not just one.* It may be that we all have more intellectual capacities than we realise.

- *We all have these different intellectual capacities to differing extents.* Some people have a great capacity for logical deductive reasoning or for mathematical analysis. Others have strong capacities for musical composition or understanding, others for visual ideas and design.
- *For many people some modes are more important than others.* Some modes are more defining of their intelligence than others. This is easy to see in people who have found their natural strengths.
- *High abilities in one area do not entail high abilities in others.* A good mathematician may be just that. It doesn't follow that he or she should have comparable abilities elsewhere, as a painter, chemist or business leader for example.

There are not two types of people, academic or non-academic, but many. Rather than seeing people as more or less intelligent on a single scale, we should think of all individuals having an array of intellectual capacities, an intelligence profile. These principles are largely ignored in the explicit hierarchy of subjects in our schools. I remember some years ago having a public debate with a leading advocate of visual arts education. Art is an essential part of a balanced education. But he was arguing rather more than this. He said that art is more important than dance and drama: that art – but not dance and drama – should be compulsory in schools. I asked him why and he said that 80 per cent of information about the world comes to us through our eyes. I'm always amused by these sorts of statistics. Why 80 per cent, why not 82 per cent? What if you squint, or you're blind? Are blind people less intelligent than the sighted?

This argument typifies two common tendencies. People argue for what they do as if it were everything to everybody rather than something particular to them. This is a direct product of our tendency to over-specialisation. Second, one of the outcomes of academic education is a fear of the body, or at least a detachment from it. Academics tend to be disembodied. Academic education is focused on developments from the neck upwards. One result is that people think of their bodies as a form of transport for their heads. Evidence of this disembodiment can be found on any residential academic conference when the discotheque strikes up. The self-conscious writhings of middle-aged academics are clear evidence that sustained academic work can promote out of body experiences. This is not true of everyone, and especially not of dancers. Try telling a dancer that art is more important than dance. Dancers dance because of the unique energies that dance reveals within them, above and below the neckline. Dance puts them in touch with vital aspects of their own intelligences, and connects them with themselves. The same is true of mathematics for mathematicians and music for musicians.

George Koltanowski made his mark on the world of chess by virtue not so much of his playing strength (though he was made an honorary grandmaster in 1988) as for his extraordinary memory, which enabled him to play a large number of games simultaneously without sight of the board. He could also conduct a blindfold *knight's tour* in which a chess knight covers the whole board using legal moves but using each square only once. He embellished such public performances with curious extra details such as performing the feat over three boards or writing additional information on squares. He fills in the squares with names, phone numbers, banknotes, serial numbers and the like, given him by the audience. He then takes a few minutes (often less than three) to completely memorise the board and then does the knight's tour by hopping from one item to another. His true ambition was in the world of blindfold chess. In 1931 he set a world record by scoring 25 points from a possible 30 in an exhibition at Antwerp. Over two and half hours, without sight of any of the boards, he won 20 games and drew 10. Even in his fifties, he continued to set a world record in the realm of blindfold play. In December 1960 he played against 56 opponents consecutively at the rate of ten seconds per move for more than 9¾ hours. He conducted the entire display blindfold and he did not lose a single game, winning 50 and drawing six.[51]

I worked once with Robert Cohan the gifted partner of Martha Graham and founder director of the London School of Contemporary Dance. I asked him about the process of choreography. Dancers, he told me, think physically. It isn't that they begin from a verbal proposition and try to dance it. Choreography evolves in the making. It is a material process of movement and reflection on movement. It is important to understand the material process of creativity and we will focus on it more in the next chapter. I asked Bob Cohan how he came to contemporary dance. In the early 1950s he left the US army and was living in New York. He had always enjoyed dancing and had a conventional training. A friend told him of a woman who was running dance classes downtown and suggested he might enjoy them. He went, and his life was changed. After the first three-hour session with Martha Graham, his body was shaking almost uncontrollably with excitement. He discovered in her methods and forms of dance a capacity in himself that he had never suspected. Through meeting Martha Graham he found himself and he spent his artistic life in the world he helped her eventually to create.[52]

Does all of this mean that no one can be thought of as more intelligent that anyone else? Clearly not. But the idea of plural intelligence means we have to recast the question. Some people have high abilities in many areas, music, mathematics, verbal reasoning, visual representation and so on. We typically think of such people as renaissance figures. But we should hesitate to describe a philosopher with strong abilities in deductive reasoning alone as more intelligent than a person with equally high abilities in musical composition or performance. This is not an argument against rationalist abilities or academic achievement, it is for an expanded concept of intelligence that includes but goes beyond them. If we fail to promote a full sense of people's abilities through education and training, as we have done for generations, some – perhaps most – will never really discover what their real intellectual capacities are. In a crucial sense they never really know who they are or what they might become.

Conclusion

All individuals have a wide range of abilities across different types of intelligence. It is undoubtedly the case that overall some individuals are more intelligent than others: that is, they have high abilities across a number of intelligences, in music, mathematics, deductive reasoning, visual perception and so on. It is equally the case that high ability in one field does not entail high abilities in others. A gifted mathematician need not be a gifted painter: a gifted poet may have no gift in dance. The essential point is that academic intelligence is often assumed to be of a higher order than all others. Other abilities are assumed to be less important or impressive in themselves. Consequently they are neither sought nor valued to the same extent. The result is that many individuals do not know what they can do, nor who they really are. When we talk of realising our potential, we should aim to do so in both senses of the word. We need to understand its range and variety. We also need to turn it into reality. This is where the idea of creativity assumes a central significance. The next chapter looks at what creativity means, how it relates to this idea of intelligence and how it can be promoted or stifled, in education, in business and beyond.

Chapter Four

BEING CREATIVE

'The imagination in its loyalty to possibility often takes the curved path rather than the linear way.'

John O'Donohue

Introduction

There are many misconceptions about creativity. Creativity is not a separate faculty that some people have and others do not. It is a function of intelligence: it takes many forms, it draws from many different capacities and we all have different creative capabilities. Creativity is possible in any activity in which human intelligence is actively engaged. The distinctive feature of human intelligence is imagination and the power of symbolic thought. Our lives are shaped by the ideas we have and beliefs we hold. New ways of thinking can transform us. To promote creativity it is essential to understand the main elements and phases of the creative process including:

- the importance of the medium;
- the need to be in control of the medium;
- the need to play and take risks; and
- the need for critical judgment.

In this chapter I look at the nature of creativity and relate it to a broader view of intelligence and human ability. I begin by looking at some of the most common misconceptions. These often stand in the way of a realistic strategy to develop the creative abilities that lie deep in all of us. I then develop three main ideas:

- *Human intelligence is essentially creative.* We not only find meaning in the world, we interpret it through structures of ideas and beliefs. We each create the worlds we live in.
- *We do this through the power of representation – of symbolic thought.* We experience the world in many ways and use different ways to make sense of it: including words, images, sounds, movements, gestures and many more.
- *Our ideas interact with events and are capable of profound change.* If events can be construed, they can be misconstrued and re-construed.

Creating problems

For all the interest in creativity, there are also some deep concerns about what it is and how it can be developed.

Special people?

The troubled creative genius is a powerful image of Western culture. Our sense of history is populated with stories of great men and women whose visionary ideas, in science, medicine, the arts, business, politics, have shaped the world. Many companies have creative departments where all the creative people are thought to be concentrated. They are known as 'creatives'; they keep irregular hours, don't wear ties, and come in late because they've been struggling with an idea. This all adds to the idea of creative people being set apart from the rest of us by their extraordinary natural gifts. The word creativity itself suggests some sort of separate faculty like memory or sight. On this basis, some people are thought to have creativity like some have brown eyes or black hair. On the surface, this all makes some rough sense. Some people do seem more creative than others, and a few do scale extraordinary heights of creative achievement. There are people whose visions have changed the course of history. But it doesn't follow that 'creative' people are a special breed or that the majority of people are not creative.

Special activities?

A second misconception is that creativity only happens in particular sorts of activities, and especially the arts. Artists do aim to produce original work and at their best they are highly creative. But the daily work of artists involves more than surfing on a constant tide of inspiration. A good deal of what they do is not creative at all in any strict sense. It involves a huge amount of practical routine, including refining the control of materials and techniques. Watch a dance company in rehearsal or a musician practising an instrument. Writing novels and composing poems is as much a diligent craft as a process of inspiration. It's often said that creativity in the arts is 5 per cent inspiration and 95 per cent perspiration. We'll come back to this later in talking about the creative process. But there is a more important point to make immediately. Scientists, technologists, business people, educators, anyone can be creative in the work they do. Creativity is not exclusive to particular activities; it's possible wherever human intelligence is actively engaged. It is not a specific type of activity but a quality of intelligence.

Letting go?

A third misconception is that creativity is to do with free expression. This is partly why there's such concern about creativity in education. Critics think of children running wild and knocking down the furniture: with being spontaneous and uninhibited rather than with serious academic work. This view of creativity can be reinforced by the use of 'creative' techniques such as brainstorming. These are particularly popular on management courses as a way of generating a flow of ideas. Properly used they can be very good: used badly they are terrible.

Brainstorming involves more than being told to have lots of ideas. Generating ideas is essential to the creative process but it isn't always easy. If it were that simple there would be no need for special techniques in the first place. Spontaneity sometimes has to be carefully planned. In any case, creativity is not just a matter of letting go: it involves hanging on. What you have to hang on to critically affects the quality of the results.

I was once sent with 40 or so other academics on a training programme called *Managing a University Department*. In the first session I sat with seven other heads of department including professors of sociology, engineering, physics and social sciences. Just
before coffee we were asked to have a brainstorming session on
the future of education. We were given large sheets of paper and
thick marker pens and five minutes. (If you ever lose consciousness
and wake up wondering where your are, check if you have a thick
marker pen in your hand and a large sheet of paper in front of you.
If so, there's a good chance you're on a management course.) What
followed wasn't quite the monsoon we'd been led to expect. We
ventured a few self-conscious thoughts and then fell into general
conversation until the croissants turned up. This wasn't so much a
storm, more light drizzle – a faint condensation on the walls.

Problem solving?

Creativity, particularly in business, is often thought of as problem solving. There are various techniques to help groups to solve problems, and
some are very effective. Problem solving is a feature of creative processes. But it would be wrong to equate creativity only with problem solving. Creativity can be as much a process of finding problems as solving
them.

Can creativity be taught?

It's often said that creativity can't be taught. This comes from the idea
that only certain people are creative and most are not. Since you are
either creative or not, it is argued, creativity obviously can't be taught.
By challenging all the misconceptions I've mentioned, I will end by challenging this last one. Creativity is not a special quality confined to special
people and it can be taught.

What is creativity?

Let me build a definition in three steps. The first is to recognise that being creative involves *doing* something. People are not creative in the abstract; they are creative in something – in mathematics, in engineering, in writing, in music, in business, in whatever. You could not be creative unless you were actually doing something. In this respect, creativity is different from imagination.

The power of imagination

Imagination means seeing 'in the mind's eye'. Some people argue that imagination is what separates us from other animals. As we don't know what goes on in the 'minds' of other animals, this is hard to judge. But imagination is certainly an essential characteristic of human intelligence. Through imagination we can call to mind people, events, feelings and experiences that are not present here and now. They may be things that really exist or that do not exist at all. If I ask you to think of an elephant, your old school, or your best friend you can bring to mind some mental image, which is drawn from real experience. We wouldn't normally think of mental images of real experience as *imaginative*. More accurately, they are *imaginal*. If I ask you to think of a green polar bear wearing a dress, you can imagine that too. But now you're bringing to mind something of which you have no direct experience – at least I assume not. Mental representations such as this are hypothetical: images of possibilities that are composed in the mind rather than recalled to it. They are *imaginative*. Imagination is often used to cover both imaginal and imaginative thought. Creativity is different again.

Creative processes are rooted in imaginative thought, in envisaging new possibilities. But creativity goes further. Imagination can be an entirely private process of internal consciousness. You might be lying motionless on your bed but in a fever of imagination. Private imaginings may have no impact in the public world at all. Creativity does. It would be odd to describe someone as creative who just lay still and never did anything. Whatever the task, creativity is not just an internal mental process: it involves action. In a sense, it is applied imagination. To call somebody creative suggests they are actively producing something in a deliberate way.[53] A first definition of creativity then is *imaginative processes with outcomes in the public world*.

Being original

Creativity suggests originality: that the results are new. But how new? Do we have to come up with something that has never been thought of before? Common sense suggests not: that a creative outcome can be original on different levels:

- to the person involved – *personal originality*;
- for a particular community – *social originality*; and
- for humanity as a whole – *historic originality*.

The towering figures of science, the arts, technology and the rest produced works of historic originality. Teachers don't expect that of young children. They try to encourage work that's original for the children themselves. Some are capable of historic originality – think of Mozart and other prodigies. There are different levels of originality and stages in creative development. So a second draft definition of creativity is *imaginative processes that produce outcomes that are original*. There is also a third element, value.

Values

When I was a teenager, one of my cousins came to the house flushed with excitement. He'd thought of an invention that was going to make us all rich. He'd been walking down the road and was watching an elderly woman inching painfully along with a walking stick. In a moment of inspiration, he thought how much easier it would be if the walking stick had a little wheel on the end of it. Instead of lifting it every time she took a step she could just push it along. He couldn't believe that no one had thought of it before. We made him a drink and broke it to him gently. It was a good idea but for the one catastrophic flaw.

Genuinely creative ideas are more than novel: they are valuable. Calling someone creative implies that what they've produced is valuable and worthwhile. Judging the value of new ideas can be difficult. By definition, creative ideas are often ahead of their times. In the mid-1830s, Michael Faraday gave the first demonstrations of electricity at the Royal Institution in London. He stood in a gaslit lecture theatre before a distinguished audience of scientists and showed bright blue sparks leaping between two copper spheres. The audience was impressed but many of them were at a loss to know what to make of it all. 'This is all very interesting, Mr Faraday', said one of them. 'But what use is it?' 'I don't know,' said Faraday, 'what use is a baby?' A world without electricity is now unthinkable. Our lives depend on it in almost every way, from food supplies to transport to heating, lighting and telecommunications. The 19th century had none of the uses of electricity that we now take for granted. It was not that people had their homes cluttered with dishwashers and televisions simply waiting for Faraday to complete his experiments. The applications of electricity only followed the harnessing of electricity itself. Faraday's discoveries created circumstances in which the applications were developed. At the time, many people simply couldn't see the point of it. This is the often way with creative insights. They run ahead of their times and confuse the crowd.

There have been countless scientists, inventors, artists and philosophers who were ridiculed in their own times but whose work is revered by later generations. Think of Galileo. Judging someone's output as creative means assessing whether it is what it's claimed to be. Galileo's work was denounced for not being science at all. Avant garde artists are constantly asked, 'but is it art?'[54] Subsequent generations often think better of original thinkers because values change. There are many examples of artists who died in penury, whose work now changes hands for fortunes. Equally, people who were thought of as visionary in their own times can be discredited by history for exactly the same reason. Think of phrenology.[55]

Our view of the past is rarely settled. We live in a perpetual present tense. Our knowledge of other periods can never match their vast complexity as they were experienced and understood at the time. Our perception of the past is partial and selective. What we include and acknowledge is always open to change and revision. This is often because of changes in contemporary values. Individuals long forgotten or overlooked may be reinterpreted as key agents of cultural progress because of a shift in current fashion or political outlook. The strong sentiment and self-assurance of Raphael, for example, endeared him to many Victorians as the central figure in the Renaissance. There are those today who think more of Michelangelo, for his restless self-doubt, and build their image of the period around him. In these ways, our sense of history and of ourselves involves a continual selection and reselection of ancestors. History is not dead because the present is so alive.

The relationships between creativity and cultural values have important implications for promoting creative activity in organisations. We'll come back to them in *Chapter Six*. But my definition of creativity is this: *imaginative processes with outcomes that are original and of value*. Let me develop two fundamental themes.

The meaning of life

In *Chapter Three* I discussed how the nature of our senses determines our *field of perception*, what in the world we *can* perceive. But there are other factors that affect what we actually do perceive. Even with the same senses, though, different people see the same events differently. This is because they have different points of view. This is true in two senses. They may be in different physical places and literally have different points of view. But if there were no more to it than that, we could settle any argument by comparing everyone's point of view and putting together an objective overview. Theoretically this is what is meant to happen in courts of law. But it often happens that getting everyone's point of view simply deepens the dispute.

We see events with a different *sense of perspective*. Your mind, like my mind, is shaped by many different factors and influences. But they are of two distinct sorts. There are the physical capacities and senses by which we interact with the outside world. But our view of the world is not only affected by what we can perceive; it is deeply influenced by other factors, which affect what we actually do perceive: the ideas, values and beliefs through which we frame our understanding of it. When we look at a room, a landscape, the street, we don't pay equal attention to everything in our field of perception. We notice some things, not others.

If you buy a yellow car, you're likely to see yellow cars everywhere. Two people standing in the same street may perceive it in completely different ways. A traffic warden may see a landscape of offenders: a window cleaner a land of opportunity. A bird fancier wandering through a wood will see it differently from a botanist interested in rare plants. Human intelligence is not just a process of perception but also of selection. If our minds were on open reception all the time, we couldn't think or act. There would be too much information coming in, like a radio tuned to an open frequency. Even at the level of primary perception, the mind is exercising choices.[56] Our perceptions are guided by our interests, values, attitudes and beliefs. Our perceptions take place within frameworks of conceptions.

What do you mean?

I said earlier that imagination is an essential characteristic of our human intelligence. It is, and it gives rise to, our most distinctive ability: the power of symbolic thought. Language is the most obvious example. In learning to speak, a child learns that the sounds can have meaning. Our ability to connect sounds with meanings is what makes language possible. Other animals have only a limited capacity for this. If you say 'fetch' to a trained dog, it will sit up and be ready to move. If you were to talk to it about the importance of fetching or great fetchers you've known, it will sit blankly until you throw the stick. Show it a picture of the stick and it will probably smell it. Its abilities don't go far beyond the association of sounds with actions. They don't extend, as they quickly do for children, to sophisticated powers of thinking and communication. If you point a finger at the moon, even a young child will look at the moon. A dog will look at your finger. The child readily understands the idea of referring to something, the dog doesn't.

Speaking your mind

The languages we learn affect how we think. A child quickly learns that things have names. But she does something more. She absorbs the ways of thinking that the words make possible. These vary hugely between languages. In most languages there are two or three words for snow. English has three: 'snow', 'sleet' and arguably 'slush'. Eskimo languages have over 30: words for 'dry snow', 'powdery snow', 'flaky snow', 'loose wet snow with a crusty top' and so on. For people who live in a snowbound environment, there is a practical need for these fine levels of verbal discrimination. And having the words to describe these differences makes it easier to see them. It is not just that we use words to say what we think; the words we use affect how we think.

Languages are more than the names of things. They consist of grammatical structures, tenses, moods and syntax. These vary between languages, and often profoundly. The Arabian language has several hundred nouns for various kinds of camel but none for the general concept 'camel'. In some North-American Indian languages the simple idea 'I see a man' cannot be expressed without indicating with other parts of speech whether the man is sitting, standing or walking.[57] The Greek language has tenses and moods that are not available in English. These differences illustrate the different 'natural' ways of thinking within different language communities. It is relatively easy for an English speaker to learn French or Italian. This is partly because many of the words are similar. But it is also because the conventions of these languages are similar. It is much harder for a European to learn a language, such as Chinese, whose basic features and conventions are completely different.

Unlike Indo-European languages, the family to which English belongs, Chinese is a monosyllabic and tonal language. Indeed, Chinese is tonal because it is monosyllabic. Since each word, represented by a single character in the written language, is limited to one syllable, the number of similar sounding words would be unmanageable without some means of differentiating for meaning. This is where the voice itself comes in. Words are given a pitch, high, medium, low and a tone or contour. The voice stays level or rises or falls as the word is pronounced. Almost literally, Chinese is sung. Woe betide you if you sing a wrong note since the person you're speaking to would hear a different meaning altogether. The foreigner first learning to speak Chinese cannot avoid frequent gaffes and misunderstandings some more serious than others. On the other hand, Chinese does not have inflections like English, French or Italian to show case, agreement, tense or number. These have to be inferred from the context and word order. Written Chinese differs from European languages in that there is no alphabet. Each word is a distinctive character, which has to be learned *in toto* without the benefit of letters to guide pronunciation. For this reason, a number of different dialects have developed over the centuries in China all based on a common written language. The result is that Chinese people from different parts of the country may have difficulty in understanding each other in conversation yet still be able to communicate in writing. An easy way to grasp this is to look at the dial on a telephone: an Englishman, Frenchman and Italian would all understand the same numbers even though they sound different if they read them out loud.[58]

Such languages reflect quite different ways of thinking. Children absorb the ways of thinking that are embedded in the languages they learn. In this way, words play a central role in the growth of consciousness as a whole. But important as they are, words are not the ways in which we think. Words help us to think about some types of experience, they are relatively useless in dealing with others.

Thinking differently

One of the most celebrated philosophers of the Enlightenment was the earnest Bishop Berkeley. In the 18th century, he developed his theory of idealism, which proposed that the whole world might not exist at all. It might be no more than an elaborate idea in the mind of God. His theory was greeted with amusement by the celebrated wit, Dr Johnson. One of the Bishop's supporters attacked Dr Johnson saying that Berkeley's theory 'could not be refuted'. Dr Johnson turned to a nearby boulder, kicked it with his foot and said, 'I refute it thus'. To Dr Johnson and everyone else, even sceptical philosophers seem to carry on living in the world and doing their shopping despite their uncertainty about its existence.

The philosophers of the Enlightenment worried about whether the world was as it seemed and even whether it was there at all. However tantalising these problems may be to philosophers, they're only problems if we think about them. For most of the time, we live our lives in what has been called the *natural attitude*.[59] We simply accept that the world is there, that the people and things we see about us are real and appear to us all in the same way. The outer world may be an illusion but for everyday purposes we assume it is not.

The natural attitude is the dominant mode of consciousness, but it's not the only one. We see things differently in different states of mind. While some 17th and 18th century philosophers were busy dismantling public confidence in the material world, a new breed of scientists set about bringing it under our control. The scientific outlook is not so much a rejection of philosophical doubts. It is more an illustration that in daily life, as Bertrand Russell commented, we assume as certain many things which on closer scrutiny we find to be full of apparent contradictions. In the 20th century, Einstein's *theories of relativity* shook the scientific establishment by arguing that in physics some 'absolutes' are not absolutes at all: that light doesn't always travel in straight lines and that time might sometimes go backwards.

Setting aside the behaviour of the universe, we know this from our own personal experiences. Our own states of mind can bring about startling changes of perception. Our sense of space and time, for example, can be profoundly affected by feelings of anxiety or elation, by depression or boredom and of course by drugs or alcohol.[60] But even in a 'normal' frame of mind, we tend to move constantly between different states of consciousness, from the conscious detachment of religious contemplation to unconscious daydreaming; from the imaginal and imaginative experiences of reading, to entering the virtual spaces of paintings or photographs. In this respect, consciousness is like the little dog with the brass band: 'It is forever running ahead, dropping back or trotting alongside while the process of events moves steadily on'.[61]

Some systems of religion and meditation encourage a change of consciousness. In meditation, the aim is to release the grip of the natural attitude and to calm the mental traffic that fills our minds: to stop thinking and become more aware. We experience the world at different times in different states of mind and move between different *realms of meaning*. Ideas and perceptions that seem plausible in one may seem irrational in another.

Modes of understanding

Academic education, important though it is, gives priority to ideas that can be best expressed in words and numbers. But some of our most important ideas can't be expressed in these ways and some of our creative abilities do not prosper in these modes at all. Think of the differences between a sentence and a picture. In verbal language, one word follows another in sequences that are governed by conventions of syntax. This works well for ideas that can be laid out sequentially. But trying to put some experiences into words is like stringing clothes out on a washing line when in practice they are worn one inside the other. Pictures give the whole pattern of ideas simultaneously. In these forms we can express thoughts that do not fit the structures of words.

Anything may be a symbol. A sunset may symbolise sadness for you and euphoria for someone else because of personal associations or states of mind. These symbols are personal and psychological. Formal symbols are intended to mean something. There's a difference between those that are *systematic* and those that are *schematic*. Words and numbers are examples of systematic symbolisms. They have:

- separate elements which are definable in terms of each other; and
- rules that affect how they can be used and still mean something.

Words have conventional meanings just as numbers have accepted values. If you come across a new word you can look it up in a dictionary and its meanings will be defined there using other words. Systems of numbers are built from a small set of basic units that can be combined systematically to express an infinite variety of precise meanings. Systematic symbolisms are governed by rules, and sense is clearly divided from nonsense through agreed procedures. In such a system there are only certain ways in which the various elements can be composed and still make sense. We may not be able to understand what a given sentence means, but we can generally recognise that it does mean something through its meeting the rules of the system. And if we meet a new word, we can always look it up. In fact we don't always need to look up a new word to understand its meaning. This is often clear to us by its general context.

The systematic nature of language is illustrated by Polanyi who asked what would happen if we wanted to replace each different sentence in the English language by a unique word. We must first envisage he said that from an alphabet of 23 letters we could construct 23^8 eight-letter words: that is about 100 billion. This million-fold enrichment of the English language would completely destroy it not only because nobody could remember so many words but for the important reason that many would be meaningless. For the meaning of a word is formed and made clear by repeated use and the vast majority of our eight-letter words would be used only once or too rarely to acquire a definite meaning.[62]

Paintings, poems, music and dance are examples of schematic symbols. Their meanings are uniquely expressed in the forms they take. If you want to understand the meaning of a painting you can't turn to a dictionary of colours to see what blue and green usually mean when they are put together. There is no manual of chords and harmonies that will tell us what a symphony is driving at and no dramatic codebook will tell us what a play means. There are no fixed meanings for the symbolic forms of art, which divide sense from nonsense. The meaning of a work of art is only available in the particular form in which it is expressed. The sound and feel of work in the arts is inseparable not only from *what* it means but from *how* it means. A painting, a play, a symphony, a novel are complex and unique forms created out of a sense of form and cultural knowledge rather than from conventional usage.

> The composer Gustav Mahler was sitting in his studio completing a new piano piece. As he was playing, one of his students came into the room and listened quietly. At the end of the piece the student said, 'Maestro, that was wonderful. What is it about?' Mahler turned to him and said, 'It's about this.' And he played it again. If the ideas in the music could be expressed in words, there'd be no need to write the music in the first place.

Schematic forms may use systematic symbols. Plays, novels and poems are after all written in words; and there is musical notation. But the score is not the music, just as the text is not the play. These are the symbols in which the schematic work is encoded and from which it must be translated either in performance or by the reader.

Words can be used in a functional way to get the world's business done. Few of us spend much time refining the form of a letter to a friend or a note to someone we work with. Our interest is in what is being said rather than in how it is expressed; in content rather than form. But poems are not only concerned with literal meanings or with systematic communication. They are concerned with layers of meanings, with subtle associations. The poet tries to capture the qualities of experience. These are expressed in the connotations of words as much as in their literal meanings. At the heart of this process is the crafting of form. Their interest is not only in content but also in the form of expression, in the exact use of particular words and in the rhythms of the poem taken as a whole. Consider this by W.B. Yeats:

When You Are Old
When you are old and grey and full of sleep,
And nodding by the fire, take down this book,
And slowly read, and dream of the soft look
Your eyes had once, and of their shadows deep;

How many loved your moments of glad grace,
And loved your beauty with love false or true,
But one man loved the pilgrim soul in you,
And loved the sorrows of your changing face;

And bending down beside the glowing bars,
Murmur, a little sadly, how Love fled
And paced upon the mountains overhead
And hid his face amid a crowd of stars.

W.B. Yeats

It is a feature of schematic symbols that we respond to them as a whole. We don't only respond to a poem, or a play, or to music, line by line or note by note. The complete work is more that the sum of its parts. In watching a drama, the audience is not faced with reading something that it can unravel systematically by reading off its meaning like a computer print out. Like the actors and director, the audience is involved in interpreting what it sees. A play is open to interpretation on two levels: what is expressed in the play and what is expressed by the play. We interpret what is being expressed in the play as it unfolds before us, by following piecemeal the actions of the characters. It is only when the play is over that we can make our sense of the play as a whole.

I say our sense because what the play means for us may be quite different from its meaning for the actors, the dramatist or the director. The rich three-dimensional world that the dramatist seeks to invoke exists on the page in an abstract form from which it is impossible to derive the performance itself purely by logical means. Giving the world of the drama a living form involves the director and actors in a sustained effort of interpretation, which draws heavily on intuition, skill and cultural knowledge. It is for this reason that memorable performances are indelibly stamped not only with the original creative work of the dramatist but with that of the actors who bring it to life: Gielgud's Hamlet, Warner's Hamlet and so on. A written play suggests a performance; it does not determine it. Grotowski has observed that all great texts represent a sort of deep gulf for us: 'Take Hamlet. Professors will tell us that they have each discovered an objective Hamlet. They suggest to us revolutionary Hamlets, rebel and impotent Hamlets, Hamlet the outsider etc. But there is no objective Hamlet. The strength of each great work really exists in its catalytic effect. It opens doors.'[63]

We all use different modes of representation to express different types of ideas. The artist does not translate an idea directly into music or paint or drama. She is dealing with musical, visual or dramatic ideas. Different modes of representation are needed to formulate different sorts of ideas. Some ideas can only be expressed in mathematics. As the Nobel physicist, Richard Feynmann, put it:

'If you're interested in the ultimate character of the physical world, at present time our only way to understand it is through a mathematical type of reasoning. I don't think a person can appreciate much of these particular aspects of the world – the great depth and character of the universality of the laws, relationships of things – without an understanding of mathematics. There are many aspects of the world where mathematics is unnecessary – such as love – which are very delightful and wonderful to appreciate and to feel awe about. But if physics is what are talking about, then not to know mathematics is a severe limitation in understanding the world.'[64]

Like words, mathematics is best for some forms of understanding but relatively poor for others. If we want to understand the movements of electrons, we need algebra. If you want to express your love for someone you should use poetry. If someone asks you how much you love them, you're better not handing them an equation, saying 'Here, you work it out.'

Beyond the here-and-now

The power of representation, of symbolic thought, emancipates us from the here-and-now and enables us to have ideas that are not bound by our immediate environment. We not only look at the moon, we can have ideas about it; not just feel sad but capture sadness in music; not just live in communities, but construct political theories. This power results in our capacity for philosophy, religion and all else that distinguishes human intelligence and culture. Some theories of intelligence argue that there is a direct line from the senses to the brain to the actions we take. Susan Langer argues that there is an intermediate process:

> 'For the brain is not merely a great transmitter, a super switch-board, it is better likened to a great transformer. The current of experience that passes through it undergoes a change of character not through ... the sense by which the perception entered but by virtue of a primary use which is made of it immediately. It is sucked into the stream of symbols which constitute a human mind.'[65]

Changing our minds

The Oxford English Dictionary occasionally publishes supplements of new words or forms of expression that have entered the language. Some people deplore this kind of thing and see it as evidence of deteriorating standards and as a drift from correct English. But English has been in a constant state of evolution since its inception. It was only in the 18th century that any attempt was make to formalise spelling and punctuation of English at all. The language we speak in the 21st century would be virtually unintelligible to Shakespeare, and so would his way of speaking to us. Toffler quotes an estimate that of the 450,000 words in general use in the English language now, perhaps only 250,000 would have been understood by Shakespeare. If Shakespeare were to materialise in London or New York today he would be able to understand on average only five out of every nine words in our vocabulary. As Toffler puts it, 'the Bard would be a semi-literate'.

All living languages are dynamic. New words and expressions emerge continually in response to new situations, ideas and feelings. We interpret our experience within our existing frameworks of ideas. But these ideas are also tested in the flow of experience itself. We make sense of the world by trying ideas on for size. As Kelly puts it, to make sense out of events we thread them through with ideas, and to make sense of the ideas we must test them against events. In these ways we make sense of the world by a process of 'successive approximations'. This process can of course be slowed down or stopped through dogma or indoctrination. Our ideas and our words can liberate or imprison us. For all these reasons, no one needs to be completely hemmed in by circumstances: 'no one needs to be the victim of their own biography'.[66]

New ideas can transform how we see things. At the opening of *Chapter Three* there is a question that was posed by the philosopher Bertrand Russell about how we are to think of ourselves. The very fact that we can ask the question shows that we might be either according to our line of interest and point of view. We not only perceive the world, we conceive it. We not only have experiences; we have ideas and thoughts about them. The ideas we have at our disposal profoundly affect the sense we make of things and the meanings we create. To this extent we make the world we live in and we can remake it. What does all of this tell us about the nature and process of creativity?

The creative process

Creativity is a process, not an event. To call something a process indicates a relationship between its various elements: that each aspect and phase of what happens is related to every other. So what's involved in the process of being creative? I want to focus on three crucial features:

- the importance of finding the right medium for your own creative strengths;

- the necessity of being able to control the medium; and
- the need for freedom to experiment and take risks.

All three of these are essential to the creative process.

Finding your medium

Being creative involves doing something: it takes place in a medium. Real creativity comes from finding your medium, from being in your element. Wynton Marsalis is one of the greatest jazz musicians of our time. If you listen to him playing the trumpet, it's as if he is speaking to you through it. In a sense, he is. His creativity as a musician is indivisible from his passion for the expressive qualities of the trumpet itself. For him and for us, his power with that instrument is enough. We don't say, 'This is all very well but he's hopeless on the zither.' The trumpet is his medium. For other musicians it is the guitar, the piano, the violin or whatever. Our creative capacities are released and realised through the medium we use. Discovering the right medium is often a tidal moment in the creative life of the individual.

Leonard Bernstein was asked why he turned to music. He said that when he was a young child, he came downstairs one morning to an upright piano in the hallway of his home. His parents had agreed to look after the piano while some friends were out of the country. Bernstein's family wasn't especially musical and he had never been close to a piano before. With a child's curiosity he lifted the lid, pressed on the keys and felt the sounds vibrate from the instrument. A wave of excitement rushed through him. He didn't know why this happened but he knew then that he wanted to spend as much time as he could making such sounds. He had found his medium. In doing so he opened the door to his own creative potential.

Creativity can be suppressed by the wrong medium. Some years ago, I worked with a very good literary editor on a book I'd written. She was an excellent judge of style and added hugely to the quality of the book, as good literary editors should. She told me she'd become a literary editor in her forties. Before that she was a concert pianist. I asked why she'd changed professions. She said that she had been giving a concert in London with a distinguished conductor. After the concert they had dinner. Over the meal, he said how good her performance had been and she thanked him. 'But you didn't enjoy it, did you?' he said. She was taken aback. This hadn't occurred to her. She said she hadn't enjoyed it particularly, but then she never did. He asked why she did it and she said, 'Because I'm good at it.' She explained that she had been born into a musical family. She'd taken piano lessons and showed talent; she'd gone on to take a music degree, then a doctorate of music and on to a concert career. Neither she nor anyone else had stopped to ask whether she wanted to do this or whether she enjoyed it. She did it because she was good at it. The conductor said, 'Being good at something isn't a good enough reason to spend your life doing it.' In the weeks that followed she wrestled with this idea and concluded that he was right. She finished the season of concerts, closed the piano lid and never opened it again. She turned instead to books, the art form she really loved. When people find their medium, they discover their real creative strengths and come into their own.

Porcelain was introduced into Britain in the 18th century. Some of the most exquisite and valued pieces in porcelain were made in the Chelsea Porcelain Factory that was founded by Nicholas Sprimont in 1743. Before Sprimont discovered porcelain he was a silversmith by trade. He was a competent enough silversmith and made a good living. But then he came upon this new material which fired his imagination. He loved the feel of it and the possibilities it held. Over the next 20 years he produced beautiful objects that far surpassed his achievements in silver. His creative energies and his accomplishments were driven by his relationship with this material itself. Like all of us, his creativity was related to the possibilities he saw in the medium he used.[67]

There are many examples of people whose creativity is fired by particular media: not the piano but the violin, not watercolours but pastels, not mathematics in general but algebra in particular. In all creative processes, the ideas we generate flow out of our relationship with the medium in which we are working. The lucky ones find their medium in good time. How many people never discover their creative capacities because they don't find their medium? Too often they conclude that they're not creative when in truth they may not have found *how* they are creative. Not finding their medium, they haven't found themselves.

Many people have problems with mathematics. Sir Harry Kroto sees this as a linguistic problem. People don't speak mathematics. They see it as a sort of puzzle, the point of which isn't wholly clear. Trying to appreciate equations if you don't speak mathematics is like to trying to appreciate a musical score if you don't read music. Non-musicians see a puzzle: musicians hear a symphony. Those who speak mathematics look through equations to the beauty and complexity of the ideas they express. They hear the music. For the rest of us, grasping mathematical beauty is like trying to read Proust with a French phrasebook. I spoke recently with a professor of physics from California. He described himself as a native speaker of algebra. When he came across algebra at school he had an intuitive feel for it. He said that English has become his second language. He now spends most of his life speaking algebra.

Controlling the medium

I can't play the piano. I don't mean I'm incapable of playing it. I don't know how. To that extent, I can't realise its creative potential. I can make noises on it and be expressive but I can't be as creative as those who can really play it. Creative achievement is related to control of the medium. Simply asking people to be creative is not enough. Children and adults need the means and the skills to be creative. Drawing is a good example. Many adults say they cannot draw. They're right. They can't. They're not incapable of it any more than I am incapable of learning the piano. They just don't know how. The problems they face are often of two kinds. The most significant one is intellectual. Drawing is not a deductive process, like philosophy, it is a visual one.

The problems that many people experience in drawing arise from the interference of the logical/rational processes that tend to dominate our modes of thought. Instead of perceiving the object as it appears, we become focused on drawing it in a photographic way, and find that we can't. The first problem is perceptual: we have to learn to look at things differently. The second problem is technical, knowing how to create the effects on the page that the eye learns to see. Given adequate hand–eye co-ordination, most people can learn to draw, but most haven't. Like learning to write, learning to draw is a technical and cultural achievement not a biological one. These things need to be learnt and, if they're not, the creative possibilities of drawing are limited.

Most children's drawings follow a recognisable pattern up to the age of 13 or so. At about the age of 8, for example, they begin to develop some sense of perspective. As they mature, they pay increasing attention to details and attempt more realistic pictures. Without good teaching, their drawing reaches a plateau usually at about the age of 12 or 13. As a result, most adults have the graphic skills of a young adolescent. Many people give up drawing altogether at this point, often through frustration. They reach a stage where their creative ambitions have outrun their technical abilities. This is hardly surprising. Children don't develop these abilities just by getting older, any more than they wake up on their 16th birthday to discover they can drive a car.

This doesn't mean that people with limited skills can't be creative. There are different levels and phases of creative development. Some people produce highly creative work with relatively undeveloped techniques. Compared with their later work, the early songs of the Beatles were technically unsophisticated. But at every stage they made extraordinary use of the skills they had. Their creative output increased with their command of the forms they were using. There is another factor here. They understood intimately the field they were working in. We'll return to this in *Chapter Six*. Technical control is necessary for creative work but it's not enough.

The freedom to experiment

Many highly trained people, musicians, dancers, engineers, scientists, are very skilled but not especially original. There are many possible reasons for this. As I suggested earlier, they may not be working in their best medium at all. A musician may be competent in an instrument but not excited by it. There are other possibilities. One of them is bad teaching. I know many would-be musicians who endured the drudgery of practising scales and harmonies only until they could put the instrument away for ever. Facilitating creative development is a sophisticated process that must balance learning skills with stimulating the imagination to explore new ideas. Creativity is not only a matter of control: it's about speculating, exploring new horizons and using imagination.

The two modes of creativity

Creativity involves a dynamic interplay between generating ideas and making judgements about them. Getting the balance right is critical. Imaginative activity is the process of generating something original: providing an alternative to the conventional or routine. It's a form of mental play that is essentially *generative*, in which we attempt to expand the possibilities of a situation, to look at it from a new perspective.

Playing with ideas

As Carl Jung puts it, the creation of something new is not accomplished by the intellect alone but by the play instinct. The creative mind plays with the objects it loves.

Creative activity involves playing with ideas and trying out possibilities. But creative achievement does not always require freedom from constraints or a blank page. Great work often comes from working within formal constraints. Some of the finest poetry is in the form of the sonnet, which has a fixed form to which the writer must submit. Japanese haiku similarly makes specific formal demands on the poet, as do many other forms of poetic structure. These do not inhibit the writer's creativity; they set a framework for it. The creative achievement and the aesthetic pleasure lie in using standard forms to achieve unique effects and original insights.

Making judgements

Creativity is not only a process of generating ideas. It involves making judgements about them. I said earlier that creativity is not just a matter of being original, but of producing outcomes that are of value. Other people may come to their own views about the worth of a new work or idea. But the person creating is also making judgements as an integral part of the process of creation. In any creative process there are likely to be dead ends: ideas and designs that do not work. There may be failures and changes before the best outcome is produced. Evaluating which ideas do work and which don't involves judgement and critical thinking. Understanding this is an important foundation for creative development.

Critical evaluation involves a shift in the focus of attention and mode of thinking as we attend to what is working or not working. This can happen throughout the process of generating ideas: it can involve standing back in quiet reflection. It can be individual or shared, involve instant judgements or long-term testing. In most creative work there are many shifts between these two modes of thought. The quality of creative achievement is related to both. Helping people to understand and manage this interaction between generative and evaluative thinking is a pivotal task of creative development.

> This playful aspect of creativity is captured by the Nobel physicist Richard Feynmann in describing how he came to win the Nobel Prize for physics:
>
> > 'I decided I was only going to do things for the fun of it and only that afternoon as I was taking lunch some kid threw up a plate in the cafeteria. There was a blue medallion on the plate, the Cornell sign. As the plate came down it wobbled. It seemed to me that the blue thing went round faster than the wobble and I wondered what the relationship was between the two. I was just playing, no importance at all. So I played around with the equations of motion of rotating things and I found out that if the wobble is small, the blue thing goes around twice as fast as the wobble. I tried to figure out why that was, just for the fun of it, and this led me to the similar problems in the spin of an electron and that led me back into quantum electrodynamics which is the problem I'd been working on. I continued to play with it in this relaxed fashion and it was like letting a cork out of a bottle. Everything just poured out and in very short order I worked the things out for which I later won the Nobel Prize.'[60]

The phases of creativity – successive approximations

Sometimes a new idea comes to mind fully formed and needs no further work. Often the process is more complex. We begin with an initial idea of some sort, a first rough sketch, a maquette for a sculpture, some general ideas for the design of an experiment, an outline of a new construction. The idea takes shape in the process of working on it – through a series of successive approximations. The first idea gives way to a more refined version, or even a completely different one. Creativity is often a dialogue between concept and material. The process of artistic creation in particular is not just a question of thinking of an idea and then finding a way to express it. Often it's only in developing the dance, image or music that the idea emerges at all.

There is a classical division of stages in creative thought: preparation, incubation, illumination, verification. This model is contested by different scholars, but it does suggest a common pattern of focus, withdrawal and then breakthrough. The key point is that creativity is a process rather than an event. The nature of this process is personal to the individual, but it often involves waking and sleeping moments or unconscious ruminations as we do other things. For everyone, creative activity involves a combination of control and freedom, conscious and unconscious thought, intuition and rational analysis.

Crossing the tracks

Creative thinking is a break with habitual patterns of thought. Creative insights often occur by making unusual connections, seeing analogies between ideas that have not previously been related. All of our existing ideas have creative possibilities. Creative insights occur when they are combined in unexpected ways or applied to questions or issues with which they are not normally associated. Arthur Koestler[69] described this as a process of bi-association, when we bring together ideas from different areas that are not normally connected, so that we think not on one plane as in routine linear thinking but on several planes at once, not logically but bi-sociatively. Creative thought involves breaching the boundaries between different frames of reference and also, potentially, their reorganisation.

Focal and subsidiary awareness

In any creative process the focus of our attention has to be right.

Although there are always points where criticism is necessary, generative thinking has to be given time to flower. At the right time and in the right way, critical appraisal is essential. At the wrong point, it can kill an emerging idea. Similarly, creativity can be inhibited by trying to do too much too soon or at the same time. The final phases are often to do with refining the detail of the expression: with producing the neat copy so to speak. But asking people to write a poem right away in their best handwriting can inhibit the spontaneity they need in the initial phase of generating ideas. They need to understand that creativity moves through different phases, and to have some sense of where they are in the process and what to expect of there. In most situations, trying to produce a finished version in one move is impossible. Not understanding this can make people think that they are not creative at all.

Polanyi makes a distinction between *focal* and *subsidiary* awareness. Whatever we're doing, we're aware of our actions on at least these two levels. If you're knocking a nail into a piece of wood with a hammer, the focus of your attention is the head of the nail. Subsidiarily you have to be aware of all kinds of other sensations, like the weight of the hammer and the arc of your arm. It is important that this relationship is the right way round. If you start to focus on what your arm is doing, you're likely to miss the nail. If you play the piano, you're focally aware of the music and subsidiarily aware of what your fingers are doing. If you start to focus on your fingers, the music's likely to stop. Polanyi continues: 'Subsidiary awareness and focal awareness are mutually exclusive. If a pianist shifts his attention from the piece he is playing to the observation of what he's doing with his fingers while playing it, he gets confused and may have to stop. This happens generally if we switch our focal attention to particulars on which we had previously been aware only in their subsidiary role.

The dynamics of creativity

Some modes of thinking dominate in different types of activity: the aural in music, the kinaesthetic in dance, and the mathematical in physics. But these and other forms of intellectual activity often draw on different areas of intelligence simultaneously. They are multimodal. Mathematicians often talk of visualising problems and solutions. Dance is closely related to musical understanding: visual arts draw deeply from spatial intelligence. The composition of music is often informed by an understanding of mathematics. Creativity is not a single power that people simply have or do not have, but multidimensional. It involves many different mental functions, combinations of skills and personality attributes. They involve special purposes for familiar mental operations and more efficient use of our ordinary abilities, not something profoundly different. Creativity is not a separate faculty so much as an attitude: a willingness to reconsider what we take for granted.

Conclusion

In this chapter I have argued that intelligence is essentially creative, that our lives are shaped by the ideas we use to give them meaning. Creativity is a process of seeing new possibilities. We all have creative capacities but these are related to different media and processes. Realising these capacities relies on being in control of the medium – on having the necessary skills – combined with the freedom to take risks. Creativity is not a strictly logical process, it draws from many different aspects of our intelligence and personality. A critical factor is intuition and a feel for the materials and processes involved. The relationship between knowing and feeling is at the heart of the creative process. In the next chapter we look more closely at what this means.

Chapter Five

FEELING BETTER

'I feel, therefore I am.'

Robert Witkin

Introduction

Creativity is not a separate faculty that some people have and others don't. It is not confined to certain sorts of 'creative' activities, like the arts. Creativity is possible in all areas of human activity and it draws from all areas of human intelligence. It is not a strictly logical process in the conventional sense. It draws from intuitions and feelings, as well as from practical knowledge and skill. One of the legacies of the Enlightenment is a division between knowing and feeling, intellect and emotion. This division is illustrated in the common-sense assumptions that are now held about the differences between the arts and sciences. The sciences are thought to be about knowledge, facts and objectivity: the arts about emotions, self-expression and being creative. In reality there are many similarities in the creative processes of the arts and sciences. Both have subjective and objective elements and both draw on knowledge, feelings, intuition and non-logical elements. These features of arts and sciences have implications for how we should think about and manage creative processes and for how we should plan for them in education and training.

Feeling bad

There is a worldwide industry in helping people to cope with their emotions. Counsellors, therapists, psychologists and psychiatrists of every sort are kept in business by a constant tide of people suffering emotional disturbances, problems of self-image, relationship or trauma across a scale from mild upsets to chronic disturbances and breakdown. The entire complex edifice of mental healthcare in the 20th century has been built on the negative consequences of emotional ill health. There is evidence everywhere that the problems are deepening, not improving; that an inability to engage with and understand one's feelings can be catastrophic. There is little need here to rehearse the facts and scale of the emotional breakdown and neurosis that characterise our modern way of life. These problems are not confined to the clinically disturbed. In his study of emotional intelligence, Daniel Goleman included the results of a major survey of pupils and teachers in the United States and beyond. It shows 'a worldwide trend for the present generation of children to be more troubled emotionally than the last: more lonely and depressed, more angry and unruly, more nervous and prone to worry, more impulsive and aggressive.'[70]

Many people feel out of touch with their feelings. Consultancies and publishing houses have sprung up around the need to help often highly qualified professional people, to improve their 'communication skills', to restore their self-confidence and to help them relate to other people in ways they now find difficult. Goleman, along with many before him, points to the dangers and the problems that can follow from difficulties in understanding and expressing our emotions. 'People around the world are facing the same kind of problems', he says.

In recent years, there has been a new recognition of the necessity to develop the ability to understand, express and use our feelings and intuitions. Goleman describes this as emotional intelligence. Emotionally intelligent people are self-directed, self-starters, highly motivated and excellent communicators. As such they are likely to emerge at the top of organisations. Emotional intelligence is recognised increasingly as an essential dimension of personal development and social ability. The success needs originality but it needs more than this. It depends on personal qualities, being able to get along with people, being able to express yourself and to respond to changing environment. Rather than the ability to get the numbers right, these skills are now seen as crucial factors for social and economic development. These so-called soft skills have been too long ignored or badly dealt with by education.

People currently entering the workforce seem weaker in these areas than earlier generations. One factor may be, as Goleman suggests, that students in universities concentrate more and more on desk study and computer terminals. Whether this is a factor is hard to judge but, as I suggested in *Chapter Two*, students certainly work under increasingly intense pressures of competition, and there are personal and social consequences. There are wider social influences too. Modern parents are often both at work and have less time to give to their children. Many young people spend large amounts of time in front of videos or computer screens rather than playing with other children. Parents' fears of crime mean too that many children are just not allowed out to play. According to Goleman they miss out on the 'the pick-up games that used to be commonplace in residential streets that furnished children with all sorts of life skills such as an ability to control anger and settle disputes.'

But there are other factors. The ability to express and manage feelings, to communicate clearly, be a good listener, to know who you are, and relate with other people are not taught in the conventional academic curricula of most schools. For the reasons I have set out, there is instead a traditional and increasing emphasis on particular subjects and forms of learning that are thought to be of direct use for economic development. In many ways these ignore the 'soft skills'. This is not a coincidence or an oversight. It is a structural feature of academicism. The division between intellect and emotion was a deliberate strategy in the intellectual revolutions of the Enlightenment and in the cultural reaction of Romanticism. It has been compounded ever since by mainstream approaches to academic education from schools through to universities. While it would be rash to attribute all forms of emotional disturbances to education, there is no question that formal education and training have played a part, at times a major part, in the exile of feelings from Western culture. The consequences are everywhere.

The exile of feeling

The rationalists distrusted feelings and emotions. Knowledge of the real world could only be guaranteed by logical processes of deductive reasoning or by evidence from observation. They argued that feelings get in the way of clear logical thought. The Romantics trusted little else. In their different ways, both saw intellect and feeling as entirely separate areas. Descartes aimed to see through the illusions of superstition and common sense through a process of sceptical reasoning. Ideas that could not be verified in these ways were rejected. Spiritual ideas, feelings and intuitions were all obstacles to knowledge, the froth of an undisciplined mind. David Hume, a leading light of the Enlightenment put it bluntly:

'If we take in hand any volume of divinity or school metaphysics, for instance, let as ask, does it contain any abstract reasoning concerning quantity or number? No. Does it contain any experimental reasoning concerning matters of fact and existence? No. Commit it then to the flames, for it can contain nothing but sophistry and illusion.'[71]

Genuine human thought was seen at best as 'a tiny grammar-bound island in the midst of a sea of feeling'.[72] There is a slippery border of mud, which is made up of feelings, 'factual and hypothetical concepts broken down by the emotional tides into the "material mode" a mixture of meaning and nonsense'. The problem is that we actually spend most of our lives on this mud flat. In some frames of mind, in the arts, 'we take to the deep (with) propositions about life and death, good and evil, substance, beauty and other non-existent topics'. The exile of feeling is obvious in everyday language. Arguments can be easily dismissed as only 'value judgements' or 'merely subjective'. It's hard to imagine any argument being dismissed as 'merely objective'.

In the search for objective knowledge in the non-human sciences, emotions, values, beliefs and feelings were thought to obstruct the process of clear thinking, and every attempt was made to set them to one side. In the human sciences, especially psychology, the pioneering theorists, notably Freud, thought of emotions and intuitive impulses as disturbances to a balanced personality that needed to be brought under the control of the rational mind.

Freudian psychology conceives of the mind as a mental apparatus for engaging the individual with the outside world. The ego works according to the reality principle. It tries to correlate mental states with external events. In doing so the ego has to resist the more primitive impulses of the id and the moral tendencies of the super-ego. This is very much a mechanical model of mind. Maintaining a rational stance depends on controlling complex interactions of psychological drives. The individual's sense of reality is easily disturbed if this balance is upset and the ego loses its grip giving way to the instinct of the id or the repressive moral tendencies of the ego ideal of conscience.

This conception of emotions and instincts in conflict with rationality has resulted in what has been called a negative psychology of emotions. R.D. Laing and other therapists and psychologists of the mid–late 20th century fundamentally objected to this mechanistic approach to human psychology and to the negative image of feelings and emotions. They saw it as a symptom of a larger problem: that our civilisation represses not only the instincts, not only sexuality, but any form of transcendence. The assumed divisions between intellect and emotion are reflected in the assumed dichotomy between the arts and the sciences.

The division of the arts and sciences

Science is the largely unquestioned source of authoritative knowledge in the modern world. Scientific methods enjoy the claim of being factually true,

'... even if they are in no way demonstrable, even if they must be taken on faith, even if they tend to answer what are, after all unanswerable questions. Scientific methods have the great advantage in this self-conscious society of not appearing as myths at all but as truth, verified by the inscrutable methods of the scientist.'[73]

In contrast, the arts are associated with the expression of feelings and with the exercise of imagination. The artist and scientist are thus seen to be operating in different ways, and in different areas of experience; scientists are pictured as methodical, clinical and objective, artists as expressive, impassioned and creative. For the reasons I have set out, formal education has mostly focused on intellectual development conceived in terms of deductive reason and propositional knowledge. The priority has gone to subjects that exemplify it, especially science and mathematics, and to forms of study that employ it. Success in education still depends more on these forms of intellectual activity than on any other. In education there is an implicit distinction between hard and soft subjects: between those that are thought to promote intellectual development, including the sciences, and those to do with emotions, notably the arts. The idea seems to be that schools can do intellect in the morning and emotions after lunch.

The Oxford Psychosis

The psychologist James Hemmings recognised a potent danger in this split between intellect and feeling. A psychologist at Oxford University for many years, he counselled some of the brightest intellects of the day. He was struck by the frequency of emotional disturbance among the young people he worked with, many of whom had spent much of their childhood and adolescence in the intense pursuit of academic qualifications. He came to call this condition the Oxford Psychosis, which he described as *extreme intellectual precocity combined with a profound emotional immaturity*.[74] The evidence of emotional disturbance among some university students is only part of a much broader picture. Why is it, for example, that people with high IQ scores and walls of academic qualifications can flounder in certain situations while those with apparently fewer qualifications may do very well?

What are emotions?

Techniques of brain scanning are generating new insights about the interactions between different brain regions during the ordinary processes of consciousness. They are also producing a new understanding about the relationship between thought and feeling. It is not possible here to do justice to these complex processes, or to how they relate to the physical experiences of emotional change and disposition. There is a growing literature in this field, which explores these processes in depth. Let me summarise some of the main themes as they bear on the processes of creativity.

Descartes said, 'I *think* therefore I am.' As Robert Witkin pointed out, an equally powerful starting point would have been, 'I *feel* therefore I am.'[75] Feelings are a constant dimension of human consciousness. To be is to feel. 'Feelings' encompass a wide range of subjective states, from calm intuitions to raging physical furies. Feelings are evaluations: for example, grief at a death, elation at a birth, pleasure at success, depression at a failure, disappointment at unfulfilment.[76] Feelings are forms of perception. How we feel about something is an expression of our relationship with it. We experience a wide range of feelings precisely because of the complexity of our perceptions of events, other people and ourselves.

Fear differs from anger because seeing something as threatening differs from seeing it as thwarting and these different perceptions have different consequences both physiologically and in the behaviours that result. In general terms, emotions are intense states of feeling that involve strong physiological responses. Two people falling into a canal may experience very different emotions. A good swimmer may feel angry or frustrated. Someone who can't swim may panic. In both cases, they experience a strong emotional *arousal*. These are related to but different from emotional *attitudes*.

Arousals and attitudes

An emotional arousal is an intense reaction to a situation. Being bitten by a dog may provoke anger, fear or panic. Emotional arousals are associated with powerful physiological changes. In fear or anger, the release of adrenaline primes the body for vigorous activity to deal with the causes of the danger. Blood flow is diverted from the digestive system to the muscles, the heartbeat quickens, sugar is released by the liver, the sweat glands are stimulated and so on. Emotional arousals subside as the situation changes and our physical condition settles. When the physical action for which these changes prepare us doesn't happen, or is suppressed, we are left with a physical feeling of 'pent up' anger or energy. The increased hormonal levels in the body, which would have been used up by those actions, must be slowly dispersed as our systems calm down. The 'pent up' feeling persists until this process is over. If the incidents that provoked the arousal are repeated often enough – if we're continually bitten by dogs or fall in canals – we may develop a general attitude of fear of dogs or canals; a latent feeling that can flare up when they're near or brought to mind. These feelings are forms of perception. We feel them because of the way we think.

The functions of feelings

Brain-scanning suggests that the seat of many of our feelings is the more ancient part of the brain, the so-called root brain surrounding the top of the spinal cord. Rational, abstract thought developed at a much later stage in the evolution of the brain. It is strongly associated with the neocortex, the convoluted folds lying across the surface of the two cerebral hemispheres. The powerful emotional arousals we experience when faced with danger or extreme circumstances drive us to move quickly to the necessary action, literally without thinking. The floods of hormonal changes that surge through our bodies are not conscious decisions but ancient instincts that are born out of the need for survival. Our emotions have powerful roles in enabling us to sense threats, dangers, pleasures and opportunities that may be essential to our well-being.

The old brain has fundamental roles in regulating the basic bodily functions that sustain life, including breathing and the metabolism of other organs. It is involved in controlling stereotyped reactions and movements and does so without reference to the slower processes of conscious thought. As Daniel Goleman comments, this primitive brain cannot be said to think or learn. It is a set of pre-programmed regulators that keep the body running and reacting in ways that ensure survival. This does not mean that feeling and reason are separated and insulated from each other. All areas in the brain are connected through intricate neural circuitry. There is a 'continual dance between intellect and emotions, feeling and reason, which is essential to the proper functioning and maintenance of both.'[77] The fact that the thinking brain grew from the emotional is highly significant. There was an emotional brain long before there was a rational one.

In two minds

In a sense we do have two different ways of knowing the world and interacting with it, the rational and the emotional. This distinction roughly approximates to the folk distinction between 'heart' and 'head'; 'knowing something is right in your heart is a different order of conviction, somehow a deeper kind of certainty, than thinking so with your rational mind.'[78]

There is a steady gradient in the ratio of rational to emotional control over the mind; the more intense the feeling, the more dominant the emotional mind becomes and more ineffectual the rational. This is an arrangement that seems to stem from 'the aeons of evolutionary advantage to having emotions and intuitions guide our instantaneous response in situations where our lives are in peril, and where pausing to think over what to do could cost us our lives'.[79]

As we grow up and mature, the balance between reason and emotion changes, or should do. Newborn babies are convulsed by their emotions, by feelings of hunger, distress, or contentment. They express them through noises, facial expressions and movement. Adolescence, the transition from childhood to adulthood, is famously a time of turbulent emotions and mood swings. As the adult emerges from the child, there is a normally a growing control of emotion, a reduction in the tyranny of feelings. We're worried when adults act like infants, howling in meetings or crying in frustration at not getting their own way. This does go on of course. We're right to be disturbed by adults whose emotions are out of control. But this does not mean that the process of maturity is one of suppressing feelings, discarding them or discounting their importance. In the intricate ecology of the human mind, feelings and reason play complementary roles in the maintenance of the self and of our relationships with the world around us.

'These two minds, the emotional and the rational operate in tight harmony for the most part, intertwining their very different ways of knowing to guide us through the world. Ordinarily there is a balance between emotional and rational minds, with emotion feeding into and informing the operations of the rational mind, and the rational mind refining and sometimes vetoing the input of emotions. Still the emotional and rational minds are semi-independent faculties each reflecting the operation of distinct but interconnected circuitry in the brain. In many or most moments these lines are exquisitely co-ordinated; feelings are essential to thought, thought to feeling.'

Daniel Goleman

In the dance of feeling and thought, 'the emotional faculty guides our moment-to-moment decisions, working hand-in-hand with the rational mind, enabling or disabling thought itself.' Likewise the thinking brain plays an executive role in our emotions, except in those moments when emotions surge out of control and the emotional brain runs rampant. The intellect, says Goleman, cannot work at its best without emotional intelligence. Maintaining a balance and synergy between them is essential to a balanced personality. We need to see intelligence holistically rather than divisively, and its various elements as dynamically related rather than in opposition. The interconnectedness of intellect and feeling is evident in both the arts and sciences.

Arts and sciences

A work of art can be about anything at all that interests an artist. A scientific experiment or theory can be about anything that interests a scientist. Artists and scientists can be interested in the same subject: painters and geographers may share the same passion for the physical landscape; novelists and psychologists for human relationships; poets and biologists for the nature of consciousness. It isn't *what* interests artists or scientists that distinguishes them from each other, but *how* it interests them. The differences are in the types of understanding they are searching for, in the functions of these processes and in the modes of understanding they employ. Artists and scientists are not always different people. In the Renaissance the same individuals roamed freely over domains that we now think of separately as arts and sciences.

Discussing the arts and sciences opens up complex issues of definition and of relationships. Science covers an enormous range of disciplines and fields of interest, from the natural sciences to the physical, to the study of human personality and social systems. The arts, too, cover a huge range of practices, styles and traditions both historically and in different cultures: from the fine arts to craft and design, to traditional folk arts. For the sake of this discussion, let me compare the extremes of each spectrum: the physical sciences, which are concerned with the inanimate world, and the fine arts which are concerned with expressing human sensibilities.

The work of science

The main process of science is *explanation*. Scientists are concerned with understanding how the world works in terms of itself. Science aims to produce systematic explanations of events, which can be verified by evidence. The implicit assumption is that it is possible to develop 'a theory of everything' and that individual scientists are all contributing to a collaborative mosaic of explanatory ideas. Scientists aim to stand outside the events they are investigating and to produce knowledge that is independent of them: knowledge that would be true for whoever repeated their observations. The dominant mode of scientific understanding is logico-deductive reasoning and propositional knowledge.

The work of art

The main process of art is *description*. Artists are involved in expressing and describing the *qualities* of experience. The poet writing of love or melancholy is trying to articulate a state of personal being: a mood or sensibility. Similarly, a composer may try to capture a feeling in music. They are also trying to invoke the sense of feeling in others. Artists are concerned with understanding the world in terms of their own perceptions of it: with expressing feelings, with imagining alternatives and with making objects that express these ideas. At the heart of the arts is the artefact. Artists make objects and events as objects of contemplation. Composers make music, painters make images, dancers make dances, and writers produce books, plays, novels and poems. The artist is not concerned with systematic explanation but with producing unique schematic forms of expression that aim to capture the qualities of human experience.

Objectivity and subjectivity

In the Middle Ages, scientists and the population believed that the sun moved round the earth. They saw it happen every day. Their conclusion was perfectly objective and completely wrong. Objectivity is no guarantee of truth. Scientific arguments may be 'objective'. This doesn't mean they are true. It's perfectly possible to be objective and wrong. Objective meanings are those that are tested using criteria that are agreed by particular communities. Scientists use methods and criteria that are agreed within the communities of science. This does not mean that objective meanings are impersonal: nor can they be. They are not *im*personal: they are *inter*-personal. This does not guarantee that they correspond with the way things are. The reason is that, 'the world of objective knowledge is man-made.'[80] Scientific knowledge is subject to revision as new evidence comes to light or new ideas emerge. Scientific understanding is the product of the creative mind.

The subjectivity of science

The sciences are often assumed to be above reproach, beyond social influence, 'conceived in the rarefied atmosphere of purely scientific inquiry by some process of immaculate conception'.[81] The reality is rather different. Science is the work of living, breathing human beings. The apparently impersonal process of scientific inquiry involves a very personal commitment by the scientist in four ways:

- in the initial choice of problems;
- in accepting the methods of scientific inquiry;
- in exercising personal judgement; and
- in accepting standards of objectivity.

Whose problem is this?

One of the scientist's first moves is to identify an area of inquiry, a set of problems, which engages his or her interest. This decision may be wrapped in a web of personal interests and motivations. The history of science is one of individuals becoming passionately engaged in specific issues that draw their personal energies. Michael Polanyi talks of the 'intellectual passions' of science. Passions are expressions of value. Positive passions mean that something is important to us. The excitement of the scientist making a discovery, 'is an intellectual passion telling us that something is precious and more particularly that it is precious to science.'[82] This excitement is not a by-product of scientific investigation but part of the process itself: an essential personal commitment to the issues being investigated.

Structures of ideas

Scientists, like everyone else, are rational only to the extent that the conceptions to which they are committed are true. Just as Descartes accepted the assumptions of mathematics and geometry, scientists accept the legitimacy of certain methods and modes of procedure. All scientists identify themselves with particular frameworks of interpretation and rely on their reliability. The astronomer 'presupposes the validity of mathematics, the mathematician, the validity of logic and so on.'[83]

> Descartes wanted to see through common-sense assumptions of knowledge to achieve a more rational understanding of the world. His method was to substitute one set of assumptions with another, in this case the principles of deductive reasoning of mathematics and geometry. He wrote in his *Discourse on Method*: 'The long chains of simple and easy reasoning is by which geometers are accustomed to reach their conclusions of their most difficult demonstrations – leading me to imagine that all things to the knowledge of which man is competent are mutually connected in the same way.'[84]

The whole framework of scientific inquiry would collapse if these structures were proved faulty. The great paradigm shifts in scientific understanding described by Thomas Kuhn have come about when the existing, dominant structures of thought have proved inadequate.

Personal judgement

Although scientists accept such frameworks, the course of any particular scientific inquiry is not determined by them. Scientists need to formulate hypotheses and to design experiments. In doing so they exercise considerable personal judgement. And when all the statistics have been coded and calculated, the columns and data carefully set out on the computer screen, there is still a need to analyse and interpret them – to give them meaning. The process of personal judgement is one of discrimination, recognising responses and experiences of being of this or that type, or as belonging to this or that category. At the heart of all scientific undertakings there is an element of personal judgement, which cannot be eradicated. It would be hard to explain why it should be. The capacity for personal judgement is probably the most sensitive instrument a scientist has available.

> Chemistry, for example, alleges that the millions of different compounds are composed of a smaller number, about 100, of persistent and identical chemical elements:
>
> > 'Since each element has a name and characteristic symbol attached to it, we can write down the composition of any compound in terms of the elements it contains. To classify things in terms of features for which we have names, as we do in talking about things, requires the same kind of connoisseurship as the naturalist must have for identifying specimens of plants or animals. Thus the art of speaking precisely, by applying a rich vocabulary exactly, resembles the delicate discrimination practised by the expert taxonomist.'
> >
> > *Michael Polanyi*

Beyond reason – the limits of logic

I remember when I was in the sixth form having various arguments with a friend, Allen. Like Mr Spock in *Star Trek* he often contradicted an argument by saying that it wasn't logical. I asked him one day why he had such confidence in logic. He was stumped. He couldn't say. He'd simply come to think of logic as the only way to think. It is often assumed that this is the case and that science and mathematics are the best practical examples. But do scientists limit themselves to logical analysis? Logic is one of the methods that scientists use at key points in the process of scientific inquiry. But there are others that are not logical at all. Intuition can be equally important to scientific investigation.

Mind the gap

Discovery in science often results from unexpected leaps of imagination: the sudden jumping of a logical gap, in which the solution to a problem is illuminated by a new insight, a new association of ideas or a vision of unforeseen possibilities. There is a point in scientific inquiry where logic is not the best instrument. Many of the great discoveries were made intuitively. Scientists don't always move along a logical path. They may sense a solution or discovery intuitively before an experiment has been done and then design tests to see if the hypothesis can be confirmed or proved wrong. Every attempt is then made to be as methodical as possible. But although rational analysis plays a part, it is only part of the real process of science.

The logic of beauty

I once asked a professor of mathematics how he assesses PhDs in pure maths. 'Presumably they're right', I said. You'd be depressed if you'd spent three or four years completing a PhD in pure maths and it was marked wrong. 'Eight out of ten: see me.' 'No', he said, 'they're normally right'. Normally. 'So how do you assess one', I asked. 'Well originality is a key factor', he said. 'Like all PhDs, it has to break new ground and tell us something we didn't know before. But the other key factor is aesthetic. It is the elegance of the proof, the beauty of the argument.' This is because mathematics deals with relations in the nature of the world. There is a strong expectation that the more elegant the proof, the more likely it is to correspond to the truths of nature. The aesthetic dimension of science is a powerful motivating factor for scientists, just as it is for mathematicians, musicians, painters and poets. For mathematicians, the aesthetic appeal of numbers is as powerful as that of a musical instrument to a musician.

Successive approximations

The essential process of science has always been one of argument and debate and re-evaluations of established ideas, of new insights or information, and of challenging and building on existing knowledge. This is the intellectual excitement and creative impulse of science. It is concerned not only with facts but with what count as facts; not only with observation but with explanation, with interpretation and with meaning.

The objectivity of art

Artists don't spend their days in a state of emotional ferment. There is an important difference between expressing feelings through the arts and simply giving vent to them. The process of the arts is one of creating artefacts, material forms. Through these we don't just express feelings but ideas about feelings, not just ideas but feelings about ideas. The process of the arts is to give shape, coherence and meaning to the life of feeling. Creativity in the arts, as in the sciences, requires control of materials and ideas. Artists bring great craft to the work they do in honing the exact forms of expression. I mentioned in *Chapter Four* the role of critical judgements in both the production and reception of works of art. There are often disagreements in the judgements people make about works of art according to their own tastes, cultural values and preoccupations. The significance of a work of art can't be measured with a slide rule. This doesn't mean that it can't be assessed. There is a difference between unsubstantiated personal opinion and reasoned judgements. Objectivity means that judgements are being made according to criteria that are publicly available and with reference to evidence in the work itself. In this sense, it is as legitimate to talk about the objective processes of making and understanding art as it is about any other processes.

Artists are dealing with ideas and insights that are as profound, as important and as substantive as those that are dealt with in science. To assume that artistic judgements are simply personal opinion is as mistaken as assuming that all scientific opinion is undisputed fact. Meaning and interpretation are at the heart of all creative processes.

The stuff from the bucket

Creative processes draw from all areas of human consciousness. They are not strictly logical nor are they wholly emotional. The reason why creativity often proceeds by intuitive leaps is precisely that it draws from areas of mind and consciousness that are not wholly regulated by rational thought. In the creative state, we can access these different areas of our minds. This is why ideas often come to mind without our thinking about them: why it's often better to sleep on a problem or put it, as we say, to 'the back of our minds'. There we can let the non-rational processes of thought mull it over and deliver a solution unbidden to us. Our best ideas may come to us when we're not thinking about them. This is true in science, in mathematics and in all fields of activity. It is no less true in the arts. In the creative state we can experience a shift in consciousness. We may experience an absolute absorption in the task at hand and a resulting change in our sense of time. As the writer E.M. Forster said, in the creative state we are taken out of ourselves. We let down a bucket into our subconscious and draw up something that is normally beyond our reach. The artist, says Forster,

> '… mixes this thing with his normal experiences and out of the mixture he makes a work of art. The creative process employs much technical ingenuity and worldly knowledge; it may profit by critical standards, but mixed up with it is this stuff from the bucket., which is not procurable on demand.'[85]

There is a sense in which the form of the work, its sensual qualities, is designed to embody the feeling it is expressing. An Impressionist painter or watercolorist is trying to capture the sense of the object. Artists may express ideas on any topic that interests them. These may be social or political ideas, especially in drama, film or literature because these deal directly with the actions of people and their motivations. They may be equally interested in formal questions and ideas about their own disciplines. This was one of the driving concerns of modernism in music, theatre, literature and in painting: for example formalism, conceptualism and cubism and all the rest were concerned to explore the nature and limits of art forms themselves.

Creativity is not a purely intellectual process. It is enriched by other capacities and in particular by feelings, intuition and by a playful imagination.

In the flow

The term 'flow' has been used to describe peak creative performances. These are times when we are immersed in something that completely engages our creative capabilities and draws equally from our knowledge, feelings and intuitive powers. These peak performances typically occur when someone is working in their element at the peak of their performance. In this respect, creativity involves particular attitudes and being able to access deep personal resources. There is a further factor, which is difficult to describe. Perhaps the best word for this is passion. People who have achieved great things in a given field are often driven by a love for it, a passion for the nature of the processes involved.

Although discoveries are often associated with particular scientists, they are not seen as unique to them in the way the paintings are to the artist who produce them. In 1959, Watson and Crick discovered DNA and described its structure as the building blocks of life. Although they were the first to discover DNA, they were not responsible for it being there in the first place. Any scientist who follows the same route of inquiry and calculations as another will reach the same conclusions. If not, there would be concern about the evidence or procedures. In Western cultures, the same is not true of the arts. Two or more artists would almost certainly produce different outcomes from the same starting point. Mathematicians or scientists may be the first to produce particular intellectual work: painters, poets or dancers are the only ones to produce the work. It is always unique to them. Artistic work is personal in a sense that is not true of equations and calculations in mathematics, which can be replicated without detracting from the integrity of the results. On the contrary, the ability to replicate results is seen as fundamental to the validity of mathematical and scientific propositions. It's because artists' works are unique to them that biographical enquiries are interesting to academics.

Many of the assumed dichotomies between the arts and the sciences are false. Both have objective and subjective elements: both involve some sort of personal engagement and both have creative elements. Both affect our understanding of the world and how we see ourselves. Changes in feeling come from changes in understanding as well as changes in circumstances. Science as well as the arts can have considerable influence on how we feel about the world and on the world we have feelings about. The arts have a positive significance and value in two ways:

- they give status and a positive place to the world of feeling; and
- they are the primary ways in which we express and give form to feelings.

There are closer connections between the processes of the arts and sciences than is commonly thought. The recognition of these connections is leading to a wave of collaborative projects between the arts and sciences. We'll come back to these collaborations in the next chapter. For the past 300 years there has been a tension between the worldviews that emanate from the rationalist philosophies of the Enlightenment, and those that come from Romanticism and the world of feeling. A common theme is a commitment to individualism. But there are two different views of how a person becomes an individual. These have different implications for the education of intellect and emotions and for the development of creativity.

Two types of people?

Throughout the history of state education there has been a contest between the mainstream view that 'reason' and 'objective' knowledge should dominate education, and those who have argued for forms of education based on personal development and the expression of feelings. These views have come respectively from the rationalist traditions of the Enlightenment and the expressive traditions of Romanticism. They have led to two different concepts of individualism. Both have compounded the division of intellect and emotion. This tension is evident not only in education. It bubbles up in many different ways in Western culture at large.

The rational individual

The rational individual is conceived of as possessing certain qualities of mind, and these are what education should promote. The individual becomes educated and independent by developing the capacity for disciplined, rational thought. It is in this way that the most reliable knowledge of oneself and of the material world can be developed.

In the natural sciences such as biology, rationalism in the 18th and 19th centuries led to a rejection of vitalist assumptions. It was argued that a rational biological science should make no metaphysical assumptions, but should explain the origins and functions of life in purely material terms. Darwin's theory of natural selection remains a prime example of this attitude. In the human sciences, such as psychology, there was in the 19th and 20th centuries a rejection of religious ideas and transcendentalism. Pioneer psychologists including Skinner, Pavlov and Watson set out to examine human behaviour in ways that set aside all ideas about immaterial spirit or souls. In modern philosophy, the influence of rational logical process of thought has been equally profound. Modern philosophers have put aside metaphysical assumptions. They emphasise the powers of logic and of the objective intellect above those of intuition and belief.

There are many differences in the various systems of philosophy and scientific investigations that have evolved within the rationalist view of the world. For all their differences they share two common characteristics:

- they are essentially intellectual – that is, they are based on the assumption that logico-deductive reason is the principal way of acquiring knowledge; and
- they emphasise the idea that true, objective knowledge can be independent of social values and personal feelings.

Approaches to education based on rational individualism make three important assumptions:

- *The education of mind.* Education should mainly consist of processes that promote a rational state of mind. The emphasis is on logico-deductive reason and propositional knowledge.
- *Bodies of knowledge.* Rationality is achieved through acquiring bodies of knowledge. Education should consist of initiating young people into understanding these existing bodies of knowledge and understanding.
- *Education as transmission.* The role of teachers is to teach children about these bodies of knowledge.

It would be wrong to identify rational individualism completely with the academic traditions of education, but there is a very strong clear relationship between them.

The natural individual

Natural individualism makes completely different assumptions. Every child is thought to be by nature a unique individual. Each child has distinctive, inborn abilities. Education should provide experiences that will draw out these qualities rather than suppress them with the values and ideas of the adult world. Education should not be knowledge-based but child-centred. Like those of rational individualism, the social roots of natural individualism run deep.

At the centre of 18th century Romanticism was the idea of the natural world. In 1780, Jacques Rousseau published *'Emile'* in which he argued for a new approach to education. He wanted an education based on play, games and pleasure, that didn't impose adult values on young minds but cherished childhood. Other pioneers of education in the next 200 years argued for the importance of play and creativity in education, including Froebel, Pestalozzi, Montessori and John Dewey. For them, it was vital for education to encourage the development of children's natural abilities and personalities: to develop their feelings and emotions as well as their intellect. At first, these were isolated innovations. But in the 1920s and 1930s more liberal ideas began to influence mainstream education policy.

A report on primary school education in the UK in 1931[86] said that education had to look to the whole child. It emphasised the importance of play, self-expression and creative activities which, it said, 'if the psychologists are right are so closely associated with the development of perceptions and feelings.' The dominant tendency to see the school curriculum as a jigsaw of separate subjects had to be questioned. So did presenting work to children simply as lessons to be mastered. Education had to start from the experience, curiosity and the awakening powers of children themselves.

Throughout the last 100 years there has been a continuous thread of people pressing for more creative and expressive approaches to education. The value of play and of expressive activity has been recognised by philosophers back to Plato and Aristotle. But the 19th century had a new perspective. Darwin's theories of evolution had made human development a subject of scientific study. All human behaviour was assumed to relate to the survival of the species. Since babies and children spend so much time playing, it must have some biological function. In the US, John Dewey developed new methods of teaching at his Laboratory School. At the Dalton School in New York and the Porter school in Missouri, other teachers were encouraging learning by doing. So too were progressive educators in the UK and in Russia. These ideas were part of a broader movement in the 1930s to encourage creativity and self-expression in schools. While John Dewey was promoting more liberal approaches in the US, A.S. Makarenko was developing his own system in Russia. The revolution had left millions of children orphaned and homeless. Makarenko devised a system of education based on practical work and collective responsibility. Recognising the appalling emotional suffering of the children, he found tremendous value for them in creative activities, beauty and pleasure. He organised music groups and productions of plays and dance.

Rousseau, Froebel, Montessori and Dewey based their work on the assumption that children should be allowed to follow a natural pattern of development rather than a standard course of instruction. Like a sculptor, the teaching was encouraged to follow the natural grain of the child's personality slowly revealing the individual within. In natural individualism there is a concern not only with intellectual development but with emotional and physical growth. Naturalist attitudes gained ground in education during the 1950s and 1960s, partly because they were seen as representing a more egalitarian approach to education. Naturalists argued that academic education marginalised feelings, intuition, aesthetic sensibility and creativity – the very qualities that make human beings human. Naturalist models of education make the following assumptions.

- *Educating the whole person.* Education should develop the whole child and not just their academic abilities. It should include processes that engage their feelings, physical development, moral education and creativity.
- *Subjectivity and self-expression.* Self-knowledge is as important as knowing the outside world. Exploring and expressing feelings, moods and private perceptions are crucial elements. So too is providing opportunities for the exercise of imagination and for self-expression.
- *Drawing out.* The teacher's role is to draw out the individual in every child, to provide educational environments to allow the child to grow into their own unique personality.[87]

There were criticisms of IQ and intelligence testing from the 1940s to the 1970s. Some of these were rooted in a concern about the growing domination of 'scientism', the idea that all scientific judgements were beyond reproach. Some people were sceptical about the authority of the scientific attitude. Others were becoming worried about its wider ramifications. Some influential thinkers were anxious that the attempts of successive peacetime governments to create new wealth were having unexpected social costs. In 1957 a conference was held at the Royal Festival Hall in London entitled, *Humanity, Technology and Education.* It was opened by Sir Herbert Read. He was deeply critical of the whole direction in which formal education was heading.

As he saw it then, the emphasis on technological and industrial development was resulting in narrow academicism in secondary schools and in a sheer sterility of education. This system, he argued, would lead inevitably to the dehumanisation of people. He hoped for a rebirth of human values and of personal qualities. Education had been based on the promotion and measurement of particular types of academic ability. It now urgently needed to do something about the rest of the child, including emotions. The ideal of education, he said, was no longer the development of the whole person:

'... it is an intensive search for special aptitudes and the development of a chosen aptitude into a particular technique. We are told that our survival as a nation depends on this partial and specialised form of education. Our civilisation is no longer primarily human. Mechanisation has taken command and the human being becomes a component of the machine.'[88]

As he saw it, the preoccupation with technological advance was turning schools and colleges into production lines of myopic specialists. Specialisation in education had been invented purely to conform with specialisation in industry:

> 'The ideal of technology is complete automation, a machine that controls itself without human intervention. The corresponding ideal of education is a human brain that controls itself free from all idealistic entanglements, free above all from originality of any kind. Functional thinking is like functional machinery: cold, precise, imageless, repetitive, bloodless, nerveless, dead.'

The point of education for Read was to improve the quality of human life. At the heart of this was a regard for the individual and for the personal world of imagination and feelings. Material prosperity was no reward for sacrificing these essential human qualities; for quenching emotion and creativity. The idea that society is plotting its own brain death, that human relationships are becoming impoverished and the creative spirit emaciated by advanced technology and commercialism provide fertile conditions for the growth of liberal education with its call for individuality and the purity of childhood.

There is a related dichotomy between so-called 'traditional' and 'progressive' teaching methods. Progressive methods are those that are thought to encourage children to express themselves freely and which don't impose facts and information on them: traditional methods are those where the teacher passes on knowledge and information in a didactic way. For some progressive teachers, comprehensive education was a determined attempt to break down the privileges of social class and to bring about a fairer social order. Where the private system had been based on wealth, the state system had been founded on the idea of hereditary ability and intelligence quotient. The eleven-plus enforced the idea of inborn intelligence levels and ignored the importance of social opportunities in educational achievement. The efforts to cater for a wider range of ability and more opportunities for educational attainment led to more broadly based patterns of assessment. It also resulted in a proliferation of non-academic courses in secondary schools.

Personal growth

In the 1960s and 1970s, the argument for self-expression and creativity in education was rooted in a concern to promote the life of feeling. This concern connected with far-reaching developments outside formal education. There was in the 1960s more generally a strong cultural reaction against rationalism. This was not only evident in education but in far-reaching changes in what Raymond Williams called the *structure of feeling* of the time. The Personal Growth movement began in America in the 1940s, but mushroomed during the 1960s first in America and then in Europe. Personal Growth refers to various sorts of group encounter activities, which aimed to explore the relationships between people and increase their knowledge of themselves and each other. These encounters often made use of role-play techniques and drew heavily on the theories of psychoanalysts and emotional therapists. Although it developed out of academic studies into personality and behaviour, group encounter attracted large numbers of paying customers to the search for more authentic relationships. Encounter or T. Groups encourage members to see the world through the eyes of others and to rethink their own perceptions of themselves. These techniques have now spread well beyond formal encounter sessions and are widely used now in personnel training in industry and elsewhere. The two touchstones of personal growth were *individuality* and *authenticity*.

'An individual desiring a personal growth experience may consider himself less emotionally, physically, or sensually spontaneous than he would like. He may be lonely and find it difficult to communicate honestly with another. The values of sensitivity training and group encounter are honesty and the presentation of the authentic self.'[89]

It would be unwise to generalise too far about why so many individuals were drawn to experiences as personal as these, but changes in the general social landscape certainly played their part. Marx and Maslow would argue that the economic prosperity of the times provided the material comfort for this sort of introspection. Herbert Read would have seen it as a response to the dehumanisation of society brought on by industrialism. Certainly people finding themselves removed from the products of their own labour, exposed to ever widening horizons through the new media, and whose roots in community life are loosened by massive social upheaval, are more likely than their parents or grand-parents to feel a loss of identity and personal significance.

According to Carl Rogers, the burgeoning of personal growth was stimulated by the decline of organised religious beliefs. It was a search for existential meaning. They were trying to fill what Victor Frankl called the existential vacuum. He meant by this the experience of a total loss of ultimate meaning to one's existence that would make life worth-while. As Frankl saw it, 'the consequent void, the state of emptiness is at present one of the major challenges to psychiatry.'[90]

'During the past 30 years people from all the civilised countries of the earth have consulted me. Among all my patients in the second half of life, that is to say over 35, there has not been one whose prob-lem in the last resort was not one of finding a religious outlook on life. It is safe to say that every one of them fell ill because he had lost that which the living religions of every age have given their follow-ers, and none of them has been really healed who did not regain his religious outlook.'

Carl Jung

These changes favoured different theoretical attitudes in psychology, such as Laing's, to those more mechanistic systems such as Freud's. Holistic therapists argued for systems of analysis that addressed a per-son's total being in the world, including the authentic expression of per-sonal feelings. The sheer expression of feelings was a key element in the international youth culture of the 1960s. Individuality, rethinking basic values and the search for experiences of transcendence, especially through alternative religions, were characteristics of the 1960s and later. The implicit goal of the group process was to live for the moment, in the here and now. The parallel with an existential point of view is clear-cut. But rather than being existentialist, much of it reflected metaphysi-cal interests. Traditional religious structures were being eroded, but the numbers of mystic and the esoteric religions and cults proliferated enor-mously. The rationalist outlook had yielded far-reaching practical tech-nologies. But there was within the youth counterculture a growing inter-est in para-sciences, extrasensory perception and, especially through drugs, in alternative states of consciousness and in transcendence.

Educating the emotions

For all their differences, rational and natural individualism have two important characteristics in common. Both conceive of individualism as something independent of culture. For the rationalists, the individual becomes independent of social and cultural influences by the power of objective reason. For the naturalist, the aim is to relieve cultural pressures to liberate the individual spirit. The uniqueness of the individual will emerge – provided there is enough creative space in which to grow. Both models are a-cultural. They also promote a catastrophic division between thinking and feeling, between intellect and emotion.

'These are times when the fabric of society seems to unravel at ever greater speed, when selfishness, violence and a meanness of spirit seem to be rotting the goodness of our communal lives. There is growing evidence that the fundamental ethical stances in life stem from underlying emotional capacities. For one, impulse is the medium of emotion; the seed of all impulse is a feeling bursting to express itself in action. Those who are at the mercy of impulse – who lack self-control – suffer a moral deficiency. The ability to control impulse is the base of will and character. By the same token, the root of altruism lies in empathy, the ability to read emotions in others; lacking a sense of another's need or despair, there is no caring. And if there are any two moral stances that our times call for, they are precisely these, self-restraint and compassion ... The very name, *Homo sapiens*, the thinking species, is misleading in the light of the new appreciation and vision of the place of emotions in our lives that science now offers. When it comes to shaping our decisions and our actions, feeling counts every bit as much, and often more, than thought; we have gone too far in emphasising the value of the purely rational, of what IQ measures, in human life.'

Daniel Goleman

The persistence of this apparent dichotomy between reason and emotion presents real problems for education and for the general development of creative abilities. In this context, the arts have come to be set against the sciences: the one apparently leading to pure knowledge, the other nowhere; the one wholly objective, the other merely subjective; the one useful, the other not. Personal Growth and natural individualism

were reaction against *objectivism*: against treating knowledge as impersonal and people as objects The danger is in moving too far the other
way: to *subjectivism*. Subjectivism is the tendency to think of individual
consciousness as separate from the world of others. The danger is in
detaching the individual from the cultural context and the need for interaction with the ideas and values of others.

> Laing describes as schizoid the person who experiences a rent in
> his or her relationship with the world and in relationships with him
> or herself. The schizoid is thus unable to experience him or herself
> together with the world but rather in despairing isolation from it. If
> this exaggerates the dangers of subjectivism, the underlying prin-
> ciple still applies: that individuality is not one-dimensional. If a
> person does not exist objectively as well as subjectively but only as
> a subjective identity, an identity for oneself, 'he cannot be real'.

Conclusion

These dichotomies need to be fundamentally reconsidered. A world
without feelings would be literally inhuman. Our most damning criticisms are focused on people who lack human sensibility. Yet our education systems do little to address this human dimension of our personalities. Louis Arnaud Reid puts it this way:

'The neglect of the study of feeling and of its place in the whole
economy of the mind has been disastrous, both in philosophy and
in education. Sensitiveness plays far more part in understanding of
many kinds than is generally understood and acknowledged.'[91]

Sensitiveness to oneself and to others is a vital element in the development of the personal qualities that are now urgently needed, in business,
in the community and in personal life. It is through feelings as well as
through reason that we find our real creative power. It is through both
that we connect with each other and the wider world – with culture. And
it is through culture that creativity is driven and expressed.

Chapter Six

YOU ARE NOT ALONE

'The history of thought and culture is a changing pattern of great liberating ideas which inevitably turned into suffocating strait-jackets, and so stimulate their own destruction by new emancipating, and at the same time, enslaving conceptions. The first step to understanding people is the bringing to consciousness of the model or models that dominate and penetrate their thought and action. Like all attempts to make people aware of the categories in which they think it is a difficult and sometimes painful activity, likely to produce deeply disquieting results. The second task is to analyse the model itself, and this commits the analyst to accepting or modifying or rejecting it, and in the last case, to providing a more adequate one in its stead.'

Isaiah Berlin

Introduction

This chapter draws together the arguments I have been making about the nature of intelligence, the nature of creativity and the importance of connecting feeling and thinking. It argues that:

- The popular image of the creative genius is of an inspired individual swimming alone against a tide of convention. Original ideas do come from the inspirations of individual minds. But creativity is rarely if ever an isolated process. There is a powerful cultural dimension. Creativity is not a purely individual process. There is an essential cultural dimension that is of profound importance for developing creative abilities.

- Even working alone the individual draws from the ideas, achievements and influences of other people. Creativity draws from networks of knowledge and ideas. Just as individual intelligence is dynamic and interactive, so too are the processes of cultural change. The dynamics of culture are illustrated by the interaction of science, technology and the arts, and their impact on cultural values. These affect the development and implementation of new ideas.

- Cultural development is not a linear, logical process, and our planning for change cannot be based on linear processes of supply and demand. It calls for a systemic strategy for creative development that involves the whole culture of an organisation and all those who are part of it. Creativity can be inspired or stifled by cultural conditions. Understanding the culture of creativity is essential to being able to promote it in organisations and in nations.

Defining culture

Like creativity, culture can be a slippery idea. Since the late 18th century, culture in one sense has meant a general process of intellectual or social refinement. It's in this sense that a person might be described as cultured. Being 'cultured' is associated particularly with an appreciation of the arts. By extension, culture also means the general field of artistic and intellectual activity.[92] A distinction is often made between high art and popular culture. 'High art' normally means opera, classical music, ballet, contemporary dance, fine art, serious literature and cinema. 'Popular culture' means commercial music, popular cinema, television, fashion, design and popular fiction and other forms that have mass appeal. We'll come back to this distinction later on.

But the term 'culture' has a wider meaning too. It is also used in a more general sense to mean a community's overall way of life, including its patterns of work and recreation, morality, intellectual practices, aesthetics, belief, economic production, political power and responsibility. This definition has been developed in the social sciences and especially in anthropology and sociology. At the heart of the social definition of culture is the concept of values: the ideas, beliefs and attitudes that a group considers important and which hold it together as a group. This is the sense in which I will use the term culture here: *the shared values and patterns of behaviour that characterise different social groups and communities.*

Most people belong to many different cultural groups: national, local, ethnic, religious, ideological and professional. Each may have its own values and ways of doing things, in its own culture. The culture of a group includes its sense of identity, its sense of what makes it a group and the various ways in which that identity is expressed and maintained. One is a shared language, shared dialects, accents, vocabularies, styles and rhythms of speech. Cultural identity is expressed in many other ways too, from styles of dress to patterns and structures of social behaviour. The arts are a feature of the social culture but they are not some separate part of it, distinct from, say, its religious or economic practices.

Living in two worlds

We all live in two worlds: a world that exists whether or not we exist and a world that exists only because we exist, the world of our own thoughts, feelings and consciousness. The capacity for representation gives me access to the experiences of other people as well as my own. Much of 'our' knowledge comes from other people and it comes in many forms: from stories, anecdotes, theories, systems of belief, and so on. While some of our conceptions are based on first-hand observation, an increasing proportion of them are based on messages from other people, directly and through a variety of media. We each build our own representation of the world but 'we greatly affect each other's representation so that much of what we build is in common.'[93] What we build in common is our culture.

> Our sense of reality is not only a function of social convention of course. There is a difference between saying that social factors influence knowledge and that social factors determine knowledge. The fact that we distinguish in our culture between cats and dogs may be due to certain social conditions. The fact that we *can* distinguish between them 'has something to do with cats and dogs.'

Any person's mental model will contain some images that approximate closely to reality, along with others that are distorted or inaccurate. But for the person to function, the model must bear some overall resemblance to reality: 'Every reproduction of the external world, constructed and used as a guide to action must in some degree correspond to that reality. Otherwise the society could not have maintained itself; its members, if acting in accordance with totally untrue propositions, would not have succeeded in making even the simplest tools and in securing therewith food and shelter from the outside world.'[94]

Networks of knowledge

There are some areas in which we can each claim to be relatively well informed or even expert. But there are many others in which we are amateur or plainly ignorant. Public knowledge is a network of ideas and information of which each of us knows only a relatively small amount. We depend for much of our own understanding of the world on the knowledge of other people. We are laced together in networks of knowledge. In large communities and organisations, these networks are highly complex. The creativity of a culture depends on how open these networks are and how easily we can access the knowledge of other people.

The dynamics of culture

The workings of the human brain are dynamic and interactive. So too are the processes of cultural change. There are 'hot spots' for certain brain functions: for language, recognition of faces and so on. But in any activity many different areas of the brain are used simultaneously and in concert with each other. The same is true of the social culture. We can talk separately about technology, the economy, legal systems, ethics and work. But they can only be fully understood in terms of how all of these elements affect each other.

The experience and the study of cultures, as Raymond Williams noted, is really of the interaction of systems. Understanding the complexities of cultural experience and identity is essential in many fields of study: in social history, sociology, culture, anthropology, and in cultural studies. The field of cultural studies is concerned for example with examining relationships between patterns of industrial development, changes in democratic forms of government, their accumulative effects on the shape of communities and the organisation and content of education. These long revolutions, as Raymond Williams has called them, in industry and democracy are also enmeshed in a broader revolution in social values which is in turn being interpreted and 'indeed fought out very complex ways in the world of art and ideas'.[95] The analysis of culture is not the study of separate areas of social activity but of the relationships between them.

The rise of the specialist

We are witnessing an exponential growth in knowledge and information on a scale that for earlier generations would have been unimaginable. The store of human knowledge is now doubling every ten years and the rate of expansion is accelerating. One result is increasingly intensive specialisation in all disciplines: a tendency to know more and more about less and less. The output of modern science is so fast, for example, that any individual can properly understand only small sections of it.

Individual mathematicians, for example, can usually deal competently with only a small part of mathematics. It is a rare mathematician who fully understands more than half a dozen out of 50 papers presented to a mathematical congress. According to Michael Polanyi, the very language in which the others who are presented 'goes clear over the head of the person who follows the six reports nearest to their own speciality. Adding to this my own experience in chemistry and physics, it seems to me that the situation may be similar for all major scientific provinces, so that any single scientist may be competent to judge at first-hand only about a hundredth of the total current output of science.'[95]

As knowledge expands, greater specialisation is inevitable. The risk is that we lose sight of the larger picture, of how ideas connect and can inform each other. In these circumstances we need more than access to information and ideas: we need ways of engaging with them, of making connections, of seeing principles and of relating them to our own experiences and identities. This too has important implications for the culture of organisations.

Culture and creativity

We do not have creative ideas in a vacuum. Creativity is stimulated by the work, ideas and achievements of other people. This is true in all fields – in music, design, fashion, science, technology, and business. We stand on the shoulders of others to see further. Let me sketch in two significant examples of close relationships in areas that are commonly thought to be entirely separate. The first is the interaction of technology and the arts, and second the creative relationships between the arts and sciences.

New art for old

Shakespeare was one of the greatest writers who ever lived. He was extraordinarily prolific and gifted. But his huge output of work was entirely in the forms of plays and poetry. He did not write any novels. Why not? It would seem the natural form for one of the world's greatest storytellers. Shakespeare didn't write novels because, writing in the 16th century, the idea probably didn't occur to him. The novel only began to develop fully as an art form in the 18th century. Before the movable printing press was invented, the idea of writing novels as we know them now was not widespread. It was not that he had a desk full of novels waiting for the printing press to the invented so that they could be distributed. The novel developed in the cultural circumstances that printing helped to generate. They included the means of reproduction and distribution that novels require and that printing made possible, and an increasingly literate public. As literacy spread and methods of printing improved, the conditions emerged in which writers turned to producing extended narratives that could be copied in large numbers. They started to produce novels. In the largely literate societies of the 21st century, the novel is one of the most popular art forms of all.

> The classical tradition in western European music evolved with the development of the orchestra and its constituent instruments of metal or wood. The modern orchestra is a musical apparatus that makes possible certain types of music. Classical music would not have taken the course it did without the string, brass, and woodwind instruments, and the sounds that these and the other instruments made possible. Genuine new technologies make possible creative work that was not possible before.

A new picture of things

At the end of the 19th century there was an earthquake in the visual arts. For centuries one of the main roles of painters and sculptors was to record the likeness of people, places and events. The invention of photography broke their monopoly. It provided a quick, cheap and faithful method of visual record. The new technology caused agonies of debate – centred on the Royal Academy in London – about the status of this new technology. Many people worried that photography could be the death of painting. Others argued that this was unlikely since a photograph could never be a work of art. The framing of this argument is significant. It illustrates the relationships I described earlier between theory and ideology. To established ways of thinking, the question was, 'Could a photograph be a work of art?' In fact, photography was in its very nature asking different and more profound questions – it was breaking the very mould in which established concepts of visual representation had been set. The issue was not whether a photograph could be a work of art, but what the development of photography meant for the definition of art itself.[97]

Artists use tools and materials. Any material, any tool in the hands of an artist, can result in a work of art. The fountain pen or a word processor in the right hands can result in sublime literature. A camera in the hands of an artist will produce art. This is what happened as photography began to develop in the 20th century as a distinctive art form in its own right. Along the way, photography came to be seen not so much as a threat to the visual arts as a liberation. Relieved from the duty to depict, painters explored new possibilities, from the expression of personal feelings to extending the limits of visual form itself through abstract and conceptual art. The period from the late 19th century to the mid 20th century was dominated by the artistic movements of modernism. It was a time when artists in all disciplines looked to redefine the nature of art, its purposes and limits.

It's an interesting feature of cultural change that for a time new technologies tend to be used to do the old thing. The early photographers tended to mimic the formal portraiture of oil painting. In due course, photographers realised that a camera made possible other forms of visual record. The instantaneous nature of photography made it possible to capture moods and events that painting could not. From mimicking painting, photography evolved in the 20th century into a distinctive art form in its own right. Similarly, early moving pictures were simply records of existing forms of theatre. The early silent movies were made by pointing a camera at a conventional melodrama. As the technology improved other possibilities emerged. As cameras became lighter it was possible to move them more easily to different angles. The invention of the movable focus made it possible to zoom in and out of the action and to create more intimate images. As filmmakers experimented with these new technical possibilities, the language of film began to emerge and, with it, the movies as a distinctive area of artistic expression. Film has also become a dominant art form of the 20th and 21st centuries.[98]

Impressionism was facilitated in part by the development of new forms of paint and by the invention of flexible metal tubes. These were both more vibrant and more convenient to use outdoors than traditional materials. They provided the means to formulate the new perceptions that came to distinguish the impressionists as a movement. It is not the material that makes art, but what artists do with it. Some technologies have faltered. Holography is technology that has yet to find a place comparable to conventional photography or film. It's a technology in search of a purpose. The new information technologies, including the Internet, are currently being used to do more efficiently tasks that we have done for many years: the exchange of information, access of archives, advertising and the rest. It remains to be seen whether the new technology will enable us to do things that we have never done before, rather than simply do them in a more convenient and faster way.

A new renaissance?

After 300 years of separation, the arts and sciences are beginning to come together now in fascinating ways. Let me take two examples: the new methods in the social sciences and innovative schemes linking the arts and the natural sciences.

Studying ourselves

Early psychologists aimed to produce objective explanations of human personality and behaviour. The hope was that they might even come up with rules and explanations for why people behave as they do, just as physicists were explaining the behaviour of magnets and the laws of gravity. In the physical sciences, understanding these laws can be used to predict future events. Magnets don't behave as they do only now and then or on Tuesdays. They do what they do. The early social scientists hoped that they could uncover the laws of human behaviour and that they could also predict what people would do. Some early research seemed promising and the results are with us still.

Behaviourism was a theory developed by B.F. Skinner in the 1920s. It suggested that people could be conditioned into particular forms of behaviour. There is of course some truth in this. Much of our behaviour is predictable and conditioned. Pavlov's experiment with dogs came to a similar conclusion. In his laboratory, Pavlov rang a bell whenever he gave food to his experimental dogs. Eventually the dogs would salivate at the sound of the bell alone. Pavlov called this a conditioned response. Human beings show them too. However, in the past 100 years there has been a huge amount of experimental research inside and outside laboratories in all aspects of human behaviour: social, sexual, and economic. It has generated fascinating ideas and conclusions. But it has not pointed to an ultimate theory of human behaviour that can reliably predict how people will act. Some of the reasons are evident in new approaches to the social sciences.

The early pioneers of the social sciences, especially anthropology, modelled their work on the methods of physics and chemistry. They tried to behave as if they occupied a culture-free scientific zone from which they could draw neutral conclusions about the people that they studied. Their research tended to picture other cultures, and especially little-known ones in Africa, Asia and America, as culturally primitive with incomprehensible and apparently childish belief systems. In the last 30 years, leading social scientists have moved in other directions. They have recognised that in some key respects the human world is not at all like the inanimate world. The geographer charting the movement of tides along a coast is not perplexed by trying to understand the values and motives that the tide may have for this behaviour. The inanimate world does not have reasons for what it does. It just does it. Scientists in these fields try to understand *how*, not *why*. People do have reasons for what they do, even if they don't understand them.

The social world is driven by the actions of people, by motives, feelings and interpretations. The social world is made of different ideas, of ways of seeing things and interpretations. What we try to understand in the social sciences is complicated for that reason. Scientists themselves have views, values, opinions and preconceptions as ordinary human beings. These can flavour what they actually see. The moment a scientist tries to understand the social world, his involvement will affect what goes on. The physical world owes no allegiance to any particular set of interpretations. Despite the successive reformulations of scientific theory, the physical universe just carries on being itself. What changes is how we make sense of it. This is not true of the social world. Our social institutions and relationships only exist in the actions that people actually take. We construct that in a much more literal way through the institutions we create and the relationships we enact. The anthropologist Clifford Geertz has spent his professional life studying the cultures of other peoples. The task of the social scientist, he says, is essentially one of description and interpretation.

'Believing that man is an animal suspended in webs of significance he himself has spun, I take culture to those webs and the analysis of it to be not an experimental science in search of law but an interpretive one in search of meaning.'[99]

Alongside more conventional methods of analysis using figures and statistics, the social sciences are increasingly using narrative description that draws more from literary forms of analysis.

The art of science and the science of art

Many scientists have deep interests in the arts: and a growing number of artists are engaged in science. There is an increasing interest in collaboration between the arts and sciences. Artists are taking inspiration from scientific ideas and discoveries and using advanced technologies to produce new forms of artistic expression. Scientists too are finding inspiration in the creative processes and insights of the arts and in collaboration with artists. There are many examples. One is the *Primitive Streak* project, which was based on collaboration between fashion design and biological sciences.

Between fertilisation and the appearance of the recognisable human form, a single cell, the fertilised egg, divides many times to produce millions of cells. Unchecked, cell proliferation leads to cancer, but the regulation of cell production during the development of the embryo ensures that the right kinds of cells form in the right place at the right time. Exactly how this happens is one of the most important questions in biology today. In the *Primitive Streak* project, fashion designer Helen Storey and the developmental biologist Kate Storey worked together as artist and scientist in producing a fashion collection chronicling the first 1000 hours of human life. Their work challenged the commonly held belief that science and art are unable to communicate with each other. Helen Storey emphasised that the most notable feature of the many groups who visited the exhibition was their sheer diversity: young and old, those with a love of the arts, those with a life dedicated to science, and almost anyone in between.[100]

Cultural revolutions

It is because the processes of creativity are essentially dynamic and interactive that the social culture is so rich and varied. It is also why cultures are in a constant state of change and evolution. New ideas in one field are likely to trigger changes in others and contribute to a constant ricochet of innovation. A new paradigm emerges when a new idea or method runs with tumultuous force through existing ways of thinking and transforms them. Suzanne Langer calls these *generative ideas*. The Enlightenment was borne along on the twin ideas of reason and evidence. These were the intellectual tools with which philosophers and scientists aimed to carve their way to new forms of knowledge through the medieval blockades of myth and superstition. A truly generative idea excites intellectual passions in many different fields. Reason and evidence ignited creativity in science, mathematics, philosophy, politics and many other areas. They had devastating effects on the traditional structures of religious belief and of spirituality.

A paradigm change tends to run a characteristic course. It is triggered by a shift in thinking and the development of new ideas that reconfigure our basic ways of thinking. Initially, there is a period of huge intellectual uncertainty and excitement as the new ideas are applied, stretched and tested against many different areas of inquiry. New disciplines and professions can appear as old systems and ways of thought combine to produce new ones. The process by which new intellectual disciplines emerge is of mutation and metamorphosis. Existing subjects regroup and other subjects take shape from them – as geophysics took shape from a new relationship of geography, geology and physics. It is in these times of regrouping and synthesis when the great genius with a colossal simplifying vision gets the best chance to emerge. Geniuses do tend to be of their times. Eventually, the revolutionary ways of thinking begin to settle down and their real potential becomes clearer and more established. They become part of the new paradigm: the new way of thinking. Eventually, the ideas that gave birth to the new paradigm become drained of their excitement, leaving a residue of established ideas and of new certainties. They enter our consciousness as taken-for-granted ideas about the way things are. They become part of the new culture.

> It would be interesting to know whether anyone of Freud's stature could emerge from psychology now: 'There might be a feeling that he was an armchair theorist who had not served enough time in laboratory routine to be a proper professional psychologist. The Freuds of the future are more likely to emerge, as Freud himself did, from a point of mutation at which psychology begins to turn into something unrecognisable to its scholarly establishment. But these mutations occur from within existing disciplines at a certain stage in any development. They cannot be planned or even directly encouraged from the outside'.[101]

The structure of feeling

Most people do not have much time for theory. Yet their lives are constantly permeated by it. The theoretical ideas that originate in the laboratories and studies of philosophers and scientists seep into the culture, often without our realising it. Contemporary language is peppered with the jargon of psychology, for example. Bar-room conversations refer to ego, sex drives, the Oedipus complex and other Freudian ideas as if these were simple facts of life rather than 19th-century theoretical propositions. Mothers bring up their babies according to the fads and fashions of developmental theories: breast-feeding or not, playing with them or not, stimulating them with music or pictures depending on the seepage rate of theory into culture. This continues until new ideas come along to challenge the old, and the rollercoaster of change begins to roll again.[102]

The world of 1800 with its population of 1 billion was not the world of 1900 with its population of 2 billion, nor the world of 2000 with its population of 6 billion. Culture, in the biological sense, implies growth and transformation. This is true of social cultures. The dynamics of culture result in an irresistible process of change. Contemporary ways of life are not only different from those of the Victorians, they were largely unpredicted and essentially unpredictable. Cultural change is rarely linear and uniform. It results from a vortex of influences, which is hard enough to understand with hindsight and impossible to plan in advance. These patterns of evolution and of revolution are not smoothly continuous. They arise in response to changes in material circumstances: from changes in the natural environment to economic fluctuations and recession, from the interactions of self-interest between individuals and social classes from one generation to the next.

Cultural change is not a strictly logical process. New ideas take root not just because they are new or haven't been thought of before. In fact this is often not the case. They take root when they do because they capture a mood. They appeal to the *zeitgeist*, the spirit of the times, the ghost in the social system, or what Raymond Williams has called the 'structure of feeling' of a time. From one generation to the next there are sometimes subtle, sometimes profound changes in the 'structure of feeling' of a culture. Although one generation may train its children in the social character, new generations develop their own structures of feeling which are not directly transmitted and which may differ in fundamental ways from those of their parents.

It is here most distinctly that the new generation responds in its own ways to the unique world it is inheriting, 'reproducing many aspects of the organisation, yet feeling its whole life in certain ways differently and shaping its creative response into a new structure of feeling.' The socialisation of the young arises partly from the need in society, 'to reach a basis of stable expectation from today. That stability depends upon the same expectations being constantly realised despite changes in personnel.'[103] What strikes us in reading novels and plays written in other times is not only the differences in practical circumstances in which people live but in their sensibilities: in how they saw things, in what mattered to them and the feelings they had and expressed. The great movements in culture tend to emerge when the limits of existing forms of expression no longer provide an appropriate framework for new sensibilities.[104]

Out of the blue?

In the 1960s, Germaine Greer helped to trigger a social convulsion with the publication of *The Female Eunuch*. For very many people, not least men, feminism was a trauma. It hacked at the very foundations on which people had built their understandings of themselves, their families, their partners and their lives. It attacked some of the most cherished ideas about normal life: that men were the dominant sex; that a woman's place was in the home; that sex was a male pleasure and a female duty; that men had great ideas and that women cared and wept. These ideas ran rampant, as generative ideas do, through many different fields. They coursed through academic life helping to recast the history of the arts and sciences. Academics revised the achievements of many men and women and the achievements of others were discovered for the first time. Feminist ideas challenged the structure of working life that propelled men to the top and kept women at the fringes of corporate life; they affected attitudes to relationships in the community and at home.

Over the next 30 years, feminism followed the classic track of a great generative idea: huge initial excitement, followed by progressive refinement and specialisation and eventually to increasingly narrow debates and contradictions about increasingly obscure points of interpretation. It gave way in the 1990s to a new phase of postfeminist thought in which some of the basic principles of the early writers were reviewed and recast. Along the way some of the most revolutionary early ideas had entered the cultural bloodstream and had become taken for granted as the natural way of seeing things. The word feminism itself, the need for equal rights and the concept of sexual harassment have now entered the language and our taken-for-granted attitudes.

There been similar shifts in business culture. In the 1982, Tom Peters and Robert Waterman published *In Search of Excellence*.[105] In the last 20 years there has been a revolution in business thinking and in how that thinking affects business practice. The whole idea of business as a field of study has grown and with it the influence of business gurus, inspirational thinkers and speakers who drive and guide the fashions in business theory. Peters himself is among the most successful. But over the past 20 years, the influence of his work has waned but many of the original ideas have settled into a new taken-for-granted view of the business world. Inevitably, new divisions become apparent as the need for new models is felt.

New ideas are not always new, and they rarely come from out of the blue. The ideas that underpinned the growth of the scientific method were not invented in the 15th century. They date back to the ancient Greeks and beyond. They found a new resonance in the 15th century and later because of contemporary cultural conditions. The applications of these ideas interacted with the development of new technologies, which they had also helped to make possible. In turn these created new opportunities for the development and application of scientific ideas. The common-sense view is that human knowledge moves forward confidently on the basis of new theories building systematically on the old. This is not what happens at all. In practice, theories are as subject to social movements and fashions as the length of skirts or the cut of lapels. A good deal of formal theory stays in relative oblivion. Throughout the world there are scientists, artists and philosophers beavering away, producing new ideas of every sort. Yet certain ideas can suddenly capture popular imagination. This is despite the fact that at any moment there may be a multitude of theories all addressing the same issues. Each might be consistent with the observed facts and be as plausible as the next one. Political theories are a useful example of this. How do some rise to dominate the others? It's not always because they're better thought out.

Intelligence testing held the attention of politicians and many educators against all comers from the 1930s to the early 1960s, and still does in some quarters. Eventually it had to compete with a growing chorus of critics but for a time it was an unquestioned orthodoxy. Whatever principles govern theoretical fashion, they are not simply a consequence of progressive development of better ideas. Other factors are at work. Theories are taken up not just because they are available, but because they meet a need. Clearly they are intended to be explanatory. Naturalist theories of education were influential in the 1950s and 1960s, not only because they were consistent with the facts of education as they then appeared, but because they expressed a mood among a generation of teachers. In the same way psychometric theories previously tallied with the selective interests of the tripartite system. The significance of theory is not only explanatory: it is ideological. In an important sense, theory is expressive.

The core ideas of the feminist movement of the 1960s had been expressed by many others at many other times: from the suffragettes of the 1920s to the writings of Mary Wollstonecraft in the 18th century. Many others contributed to the development of feminist perspectives long before they were recognised as such. The work of many of these women has been lost in the canons of the dominant male culture that they set out to criticise. Feminist ideas took hold in the 1960s because of the particular sensibilities and cultural conditions of the time. They emerged from these conditions and helped to shape them. The idea of sexual liberty has more practical application when cheap and effective forms of contraception put women in charge of their own fertility. Before then, the advancement of women was held in check by the uncertainties of pregnancy and motherhood. Feminism developed hand in hand with technological advance. But it was also part of the general politics of liberation of the 1960s that interacted with movements in civil rights, anti-authoritarianism and the expression of the individual: the emergence of the 'me' generation. In presenting a powerful intellectual analysis, feminist theorists helped to articulate a new structure of feeling.

Cultivating creativity

Let me draw out some themes from this discussion for the promotion of creativity in organisations and communities.

- *Creativity is not a purely personal process.* Many creative processes draw from the ideas and stimulation of other people. Creativity flourishes in an atmosphere where original thinking and innovation are encouraged and stimulated. It fades in atmospheres where dialogue and interaction are stifled. Cultural conditions can stifle and kill creativity. If ideas are not encouraged, or when encouraged they are ignored, the creative impulse does one of two things. It goes out, or it goes maverick. It deserts the organisation or it subverts it. Creativity can work for you or against you.

- *Creativity is a dynamic process and can involve many different areas of expertise.* The exponential growth of knowledge has led to increasing levels of specialisation. In organisations, these often result in large numbers of separate departments and in the division of responsibilities to more and more specialist roles. But new ideas often come from the dialogue between different disciplines, through which specialists in different fields make their ideas available to each other and create the opportunity for new interpretations and applications. A culture of creativity will promote openness between specialists, and departments will have real opportunities for creative encounters.

- *Creativity is incremental.* New ideas do not necessarily come from nowhere. They draw from the ideas and achievements of those that have gone before us or are working in different fields. In the same way that making original work depends on technical skills, conceiving new ideas is often promoted by knowledge of the achievements of others – by cultural literacy.

- *Cultural change is not linear and smooth.* It can be tumultuous, complex and drawn out. New ways of thinking do not simply replace the old at clear points in history. They often overlap and coexist with established ways of thinking for long periods of time. This complex and convoluted process of change can create many tensions and unresolved problems along the way. Cultural change is like the process of personal creativity. It occurs as a series of successive approximations.

- *Cultural change is not strictly logical.* Creativity and innovation should be seen as functions of all areas of activity and not only as confined to particular people or processes. The challenge is to promote processes of systemic innovation rather than of isolated specialist achievement. In the next chapter we will look at the practical implications for effecting cultural change and creative development.

Chapter Seven

BALANCING THE BOOKS

'We classify at our peril. Experiments have shown that even the lightest touch of the classifier's hand is likely to induce us to see members of a class as more alike than they actually are and items from different classes as less alike than they actually are. And when our business is to do more than merely look, these errors may develop during the course of our dealings into something quite substantial.'

James Britton

Introduction

What should organisations do to promote creativity and innovation? This chapter looks at the practical implications of the arguments I've been developing and identifies key principles for the systemic development of creativity in organisations. There are three priorities and they are of equal importance:

- *Identifying:* providing systematically for the identification and development of the creative strengths and abilities of all of the individuals in the organisation;
- *Facilitating:* providing the conditions within the organisation as a whole through which creative processes are actively supported and encouraged.
- *Employing:* harnessing creative outcomes to the core objectives of the organisation.

Individual creativity is not confined to one area of intellectual activity nor to one part of the brain. It is a systemic function of intelligence. Corporate creativity should be understood as a systemic function of the organisation. It should not be confined to one function of an organisation nor to particular departments. A strategy to promote corporate creativity and innovation should engage all areas of the organisation. It should encourage the exchange of ideas across and within the organisation and the freedom to speculate and take risks.

Identification

In the early 1980s, I helped to set up the Hong Kong Academy for Performing Arts. One of the people I worked with was a leading filmmaker in Australia. He told me a personal story that I've never forgotten. He was brought up on a farm in Western Australia. The farm was enormous as Australian farms are, covering several thousand acres. The land was poor and his father and grandfather before him had scratched a bare living out of the arid soil. The family lived close to poverty until eventually his father could cope no more. He decided to abandon the farm and walked off the land. Under state law, the estate fell to government ownership. The family moved to Perth. For years the old man couldn't face going back to the farm where he had spent his life in hard labour and where his hopes had finally died. Eventually he went to take a nostalgic look at the parched stretch of outback where he and his family had spent most of their lives. He drove out of Perth along the old road as he had done many times.

As he came near to the farm, he noticed the road was improving. In the far distance he saw the old house still standing derelict. But there was a cluster of new buildings nearby, heavy vehicles and a large commercial sign. He parked the car. Speaking to the men he found that a routine government survey of the land after he'd abandoned it had discovered a rich, thick seam of nickel running 18 inches beneath the topsoil and through the entire estate. For generations, his family had been ploughing the thin dust to plant crops whose roots foundered inches above an underground treasure. He stood and stared and then fell into a fit of uncontrollable laughter. Fortunately he was able to enjoy the tragedy rather than succumb to it. He could have been rich beyond his dreams if only he'd dug deeper.

Looking for creative ability

If an organisation is genuinely concerned to make the best use of its creative resources, the first step is to identify what they are. People join companies from many different backgrounds and with many different profiles. Two of the major influences on how they are seen are their education background and their existing job descriptions. But education is not the whole story. Many people have abilities that have not been brought to the fore because they have not been required or not valued. Many people spend their time in companies with their minds in neutral because their best abilities are not engaged by the work they currently do or by the roles they occupy. The first step to making the most of an organisation's creative resources is to attempt systematically to identify what they are.

This is not simply a matter of conducting a formal audit. There are no tests that provide a reliable picture of a person's creative capacities. Many different tests for creativity have been developed, often reflecting different definitions of creativity.[106] There have been various attempts to develop psychometric tests to measure creative capacities. The range and subtlety of individual creative capacities, combined with the many factors that motivate or suppress them, mean inevitably that all such instruments are only the roughest guides. There is no substitute for putting people in situations where their abilities may be tested differently or where different aspects of their potential are called upon and revealed. In providing opportunities for creative abilities to emerge, it is useful to distinguish two sorts of creative skill: *generic* and *domain-specific*.

Generic creativity

There are techniques, procedures and practical skills that can be taught to most people that will facilitate some sorts of creative activity. I referred in *Chapter One* to the use of brainstorming. This is one of a number of approaches that are designed specifically to facilitate the first mode of creative activity: the generation of ideas. Often the process of generating ideas within an individual or in a group is blocked or inhibited by the task itself. Simply being asked to have ideas is not enough. Brainstorming, when properly conducted, can provide a way for individuals and groups to think openly without the dead hand of premature evaluation or immediate criticism. The creative impulses of most people can be suffocated by negative criticism, cynical putdowns or dismissive remarks. In brainstorming sessions individuals are encouraged to say whatever ideas come to mind. This process continues until all the ideas are offered. Only then does the second mode of the creative process begin, the critical assessment of ideas.

There are other specific techniques to facilitate more effective creative thinking in groups. Edward de Bono has developed a series of thinking tools including the *Six Thinking Hats* method and *CORT*, a suite of practical thinking techniques. The underlying principle in these approaches is to separate out the various tasks and phases of creative work so that they are handled in a proper sequence and without interfering one with the other. *Synectics* is a system that also sets out to provide specific thinking tools for generating and evaluating ideas in groups.[107]

Domain-specific creativity

I discussed earlier the critical importance of finding the right medium to release individual creative capacities. The techniques described above can be used with most people and rely on ordinary levels of skill in words, imagery and numbers. Some forms of creativity require skills that are specific to particular domains: to music, to mathematics, to poetry, to dance, to design, to engineering and so on. I've given examples throughout this book of people whose creative achievements lie within specific fields of expertise. Their creativity derives from their feel for the materials they use and for particular forms of activity. Within any organisation there are many specialist functions and varying levels of expertise. It does not follow that all of those in specialist roles are making use of the full range of specialist skills they have. I mentioned in *Chapter Four* my literary editor whose real passion was for words, but whose training had been in music. Identifying the creative capacities within an organisation also means taking stock of areas of domain-specific expertise and creativity.

Raising the bar

One way of developing domain-specific creativity and of broadening the range of expertise on which it depends is to put people in new and challenging positions, which extend their skills or make better use of the ones they have. Academics and human-resource professionals have long known what recent research by McKinsey confirms, that the key to development is often "a big job before I expected it". Yet only 10 per cent of the top 200 executives surveyed strongly agreed that their company uses job assignments as a very effective development lever. 42 per cent have never made cross-functional moves, 40 per cent have never worked in an unfamiliar business unit, 34 per cent have never held positions with responsibility and 66 per cent say they have never had a leadership role in starting a new business. There are various reasons for this state of affairs.

- There is often too little understanding or agreement about who should be brought on in these ways.
- Senior people worry that moving people around is not worth the disruption.
- Divisions hoard their best staff.
- Human-resource executives are often preoccupied with training and other auditable initiatives.

'All companies could do better. At a structural level, they should consider what they can do to form smaller more autonomous units, create the maximum number of P & L jobs each business will bear and use special project teams to provide new challenges and ways of working together.'[108]

McKinsey Quarterly, *January 2000*

Facilitating

Many people have had the experience of being sent away on a two- or three-day course in creative thinking, or other programmes to develop their own creativity in various ways. Like whitewater rafting, these experiences can be very worthwhile and enjoyable. They may even find themselves bonding with unexpected people for the weekend. But they come back to the same job on Monday morning, and find then that the company itself is unchanged. They may maintain their enthusiasm for a few days or weeks. Eventually it drains away as they recognise that the company itself is still going on as before. Developing a culture of creativity involves more than enthusing a small number of individuals. It means energising the whole organisation. There are four particular ways of promoting a culture and a climate that facilitates creativity.

Contact between disciplines and specialists

Creativity and innovation thrive on contact between different areas of specialism expertise. The most creative periods in human history have been when conventional boundaries between disciplines and ways of thinking have become permeable or have dissolved altogether. Creativity often comes about by making unusual connections, seeing analogies, identifying relationships between ideas and processes that were previously not related. This is precisely why some of the most effective creative teams are interdisciplinary. The rampant developments in Internet and information technologies are being driven along by specialists coming from different areas of expertise to share with and learn from each other: technologists, writers, computer programmers, musicians, graphic designers and so on.

The most creative periods in the lives of organisations are often in the early stages of its work where there is a rush of excitement about possibilities to be explored and before the organisation itself has settled into fixed institutional structures and routines. Stimulating or reviving the creative impulse in organisations often requires that existing borders be perforated or dissolved so that ideas can flow freely between different specialists who are too often kept apart from each other. The point of these collaborations is not for different specialists to impose their own ways of working on each other. It is to benefit from the stimulation of each other's expertise. *Vis Viva* is a teaching and research group of artists and engineers in the United States. Joe Cusumano, a leading member of the group points out a common misconception about interdisciplinary groups:

'The notion that we are trying to bring aesthetics to engineers or conversely bring a rigorous empiricism to artists is not the point at all. The point is both of these groups do both of these things in different ways. Our group attempts to foster creativity by creating space for interaction between disciplines and viewpoints.'[109]

Blurring the boundaries between departmental structures

Contact between specialists in different disciplines can be promoted without changing departmental structures. A more radical approach is to weaken or remove such structures altogether. Whether this is practicable depends on the nature and size of the organisation and the work it does. Many organisations have found it profitable in all senses of the word to work outside rigid departmental structures, bringing together specialists into focused project teams. *Interval Research* is a diverse, interdisciplinary group of scientists and artists exploring new developments in computer technology. They work together in a laboratory atmosphere with two main objectives:

- to support interdisciplinary research and experimentation; and
- to explore where computer technology may take individuals in the future.

The members of the group are encouraged to break down the disciplinary barriers that isolate computer engineer from designer, or animation artist from physicist. The co-founders of the group were Paul Allen, co-founder of Microsoft, and David Liddle. According to Liddle, 'projects, not disciplines' is the organising metaphor for Interval Research.

'We don't have any departments or groups or structures that are organised by disciplines. We acknowledge when we hire somebody what most of their background was but the only organising metaphor that we use is a project. Everyone who works at our place has to work on at least two projects. In our organisation, we manage people's commitment we don't manage their time. In a research lab, time doesn't mean anything.'[110]

Removing or weakening departmental boundaries is not an end in itself. The point is to encourage an atmosphere where the exchange of ideas and experimentation are actively encouraged. Creativity relies on the flow of ideas. This happens best in an atmosphere where risk is encouraged, playfulness with ideas is accepted and where failure is not punished but seen as part of the process of success.

Mixing experience

Creative processes draw from knowledge and expertise as well as from speculation and imagination. Innovations often come when existing knowledge is combined in novel ways to meet the demands of new circumstances. Creative teams can benefit from bringing together older and younger workers with different levels of expertise and experience. I noted in *Chapter One* that the overall age profile of the workforce is changing. For a number of years there has been a trend towards employing younger people and towards early retirement for people with experience. This is creating an imbalance of expertise, which is affecting many companies. At the same time a number of people reaching 50 do not want to continue holding the responsibilities of full-time employment. There are considerable benefits to be gained from blending levels of experience and expertise by bringing together younger and older workers. A recent report by the Industrial Society illustrated a trend in this direction in a number of companies. The Industrial Society identified five key skills that businesses need from older workers:

- *War-horses.* The elders most in demand by the dot-com companies are seasoned campaigners with experience of previous economic cycles. One study showed that new businesses set up by entrepreneurs in their early 50s were twice as likely to survive as businesses started by people in their early 20s, illustrating the value of experience in a new setup.
- *Trusted guides.* Consumers looking for guides through the chaos of a competitive marketplace tended to trust age and experience over youth and enthusiasm.
- *Networkers.* Companies trying to build relationships abroad needed older people's networking skills. For example, firms trading in Asia, where respect for age is important, found they got on better by fielding older representatives.
- *Connectors.* Organisations relying more on freelancers and contract workers needed team builders, mentors and connectors to create a sense of partnership between people and organisations. Older people were better at providing this organisational glue.

- *Strategists.* Businesses need someone to stand above the expanding sea of information to focus on longer-term goals. According to venture capitalists, start-up firms were beginning to recognise the need for older people to bring their strategic vision.

The report also showed that some sectors of the economy were slow to adapt to the trend. In the past 20 years the proportion of men between 50 and 65 who were not working has doubled. And a third of people between 50 and state retirement age do not work. The Industrial Society concluded that the government should take a lead by scrapping compulsory retirement at 60 for civil servants. '19th century concepts of retirement have no place in the new economy.'[111]

Loosening hierarchies

The processes of creativity can be stifled by a sense that innovation is unlikely to travel upwards through an organisation or that it won't be welcomed if it emerges from the wrong places. It can be stifled by pressure from above to deliver the wrong sort of results over the wrong timescale: by demands for the wrong sort of accountability. In a practical sense, loosening hierarchies also means that those who run organisations should be accessible to those who work in them. They should encourage a flow of ideas and make it clear that ideas are welcomed and valued.

I worked recently with one of the most successful unit trust managers in Europe. Like all financial institutions it has found itself borne along on a turbulent current of change. Meeting these new challenges has called for new styles of management to make the most of the resources within the company. While the profitability of the company has risen over recent years its workforce has been reduced as working practices have changed. The chief executive describes how his own style of management has changed to meet these new circumstances:

'I have discovered, upon achieving a "top" position in management, that there is nowhere to hide. One has to make a comprehensive attempt to get things right. This for me at first involved trying to decide everything – I had to know the answers myself, I thought. This led to a series of mistakes and then inertia; indeed I fell flat on my face in the metaphorical mud. I then found that I had to admit my mistakes rather publicly and ask for help from my colleagues to get myself back on two feet. This seems to have been the beginning of some sort of improved understanding of the manager's role.

'I began to delegate, realising that actually others were more competent than me. I began to listen, rather than compete with others to produce the cleverest answer. I began to do what I knew I could do, which was to offer support and encouragement to my colleagues rather than seek to score points. I found myself gradually beginning to question and in many instances unlearn the very lessons I had spent most of my life learning, as I realised that being dogmatic is the fast road to disaster in a changing environment. Yet at the same time I found that I needed a sense of direction; otherwise it seemed that I would be abrogating responsibility rather than delegating it.

'The compass that I began to use is simple in concept – I endeavoured to balance directness and openness as closely as possible with a willingness to listen and consider positively the viewpoint of other parties. It seems in practice that it is precisely at the point of convergence of these two "vectors" that the natural way forward always lies. It is hard to find and I'm sure that I never find it precisely as I'm certain that I'm never fully open nor do I fully listen and consider. But it seems to work a whole lot better than my previous approach.

'We are now endeavouring to achieve the same balance in the firm as a whole. Admitting what we are not good at has led for example to outsourcing of certain functions. Willingness to listen has led to more harmonious senior management discussions, enhanced trust, and speedy decision-taking as colleagues have ceased second guessing each other, particularly in areas where the second guesser has little knowledge. It is also leading to more delegation and to more empowerment of younger members of staff, who often have clearer minds.

'This thinking has in turn engendered a greater sense a partnership both within the firm – reflected in the Board's willingness to create stock ownership plans for all staff worldwide who have been with the firm for more than a year – and also with our clients, suppliers and shareholders through better communication. Interestingly, it is also coinciding with a greater consciousness that we can contribute to our local community. None of this seems to be at the expense of competitiveness. I believe that our competitiveness is enhanced, I think we are learning once again as an organisation and new opportunities are arising continuously.

'It has required us to increase training significantly, particularly at senior management levels, including the use of management psychologists, and has led us to introduce 360-degree appraisals for senior managers. In graduate recruitment we are relying much more upon internships. Most of all, it is fun, certainly for me and I hope for my colleagues. Interestingly being a multinational company with employees from a whole range of cultural backgrounds has been both a spur to re-examine our approaches and a rich source of different perspectives.'

This account of an evolving management culture illustrates many of the core principles I have outlined here. The process for this company is not over nor is it ever likely to be. Cultural change, like creativity itself, is a process not an event. But the aim must be to create a company that fosters creative thinking and responses in all ways and at all levels. A creative organisation, as David Liddle of Interval Research emphasises, has several fundamental characteristics:

'It is first and foremost a place that gives people freedom to take risks; second it is a place that allows people to discover and develop their own natural intelligence; third, it is a place where there are no "stupid" questions and no "right" answers; and fourth, it is a place that values irreverence, the lively, the dynamic, the surprising, the playful.'

'Every single person in business needs to acquire the ability to change, the self-confidence to learn new things and the capacity for helicopter vision. The idea that we can win with brilliant scientists and technologists alone is absolute nonsense. It's breadth of vision, the ability to understand all the influences at work, to flex between then and not be frightened of totally different experiences and viewpoints that holds the key. We need every single pressure from business at the moment to make clear that the specialist who cannot take the holistic view of the whole scene is no use at all.'

Sir John Harvey Jones

Harnessing creative outcomes

It is not enough to develop individual creative capacities. Organisations must also encourage a culture where creative abilities are valued and harnessed to the organisational objectives. This means recognising and rewarding creative output in appropriate ways, and avoiding an atmosphere of accountability that discourages taking risks or that stifles exploratory activities in the interests of short-term gain. There is a tendency throughout the corporate world, the professions and academic life to short-termism. Ironically, these pressures arise from the very processes of change which require a longer-term view. As organisations compete in increasingly aggressive markets, budgets for experimental research, blue-skies thinking and long-range development are being cut back in the interests of immediate returns and instant results. The effect can be to stifle the very sources of creativity on which long-term success ultimately depends.

David Liddle describes 'an intrinsic cultural problem in embedding a creative research lab in a traditional-product company'. A company that creates products tends to establish and reward objectives in predictable terms; project members are encouraged to make their projects turn out as they said they would. Such a culture cannot nurture let alone reward the surprise discovery. He continues:

> 'In research, you want to do the right thing not to do things right. Productivity in a research laboratory means nothing. Creativity means everything, because most of what you do isn't going to turn out how you thought it would.'

Successful organisations need to balance their financial books. In future they will only do this by first balancing the delicate equation of human resources. Organisations that make the most of their people find that their people make the most of them.

Creativity in crisis

Like all countries, the United States is facing a future of rapid social and technological change in which many of the old skills and attitudes will be redundant. At the same time, there is a crisis of creativity, a war for talent, which is as acute as in Europe and in other parts of the world. In 1996 a national symposium was held in the United States entitled *American creativity at Risk*. The symposium brought together artists, scientists and others to discuss the conditions under which the creative resources of the United States could be best realised. The symposium was set against a mounting concern in many areas of education, the economy and the professions that national policies were deepening the crisis. The symposium confirmed the core principles I have set out here.

- A remarkably powerful creative synergy arises when people of different professional backgrounds and skills work together. This creative synergy has led to successful problem-solving, revolutionary ways of seeing, thinking and approaching the conflicts of our daily human lives, in both the arts and sciences, time and time again.
- Creative environments give people time to experiment, to fail, to try again, to ask questions, to discover, to play, to make connections among the seemingly disparate elements. This experimentation or research may not lead to an artistic product or scientific application for many years, as all original ideas and products spring from an initial period of experimentation or fooling around. This may sometimes seem purposeless but it is the essence of the creative process.
- Creativity is a basic human attribute that must be nurtured among all people, not just artists and scientists. The freedom to learn, to create, to take risks, to fail or ask questions, to strive, to grow; this is the ethic upon which the US was founded. Promoting creativity among all people of all occupations, economic classes and ethnic backgrounds is essential to the common good.

The symposium concluded that universities and school programmes are now being run more like businesses, with an attention to the bottom line that it is often detrimental to the quality of education they provide. Investment in basic science, which in the past has led to applications we now take for granted, such as computers and laser technology, is decreasing dramatically. This is because the gap between basic research and application can be years or even decades, too long for the short-term economic gain our society now demands. This perception is by no means unique to the United States. There are similar pressures affecting organisations in the public and private sectors throughout the world. Their consequences are particularly serious in education.

I began this book by arguing that companies are trying to address a downstream problem. In order to revive and promote creative abilities, they need to remedy the narrowness of conventional academic education. There is a great deal that organisations can do immediately to apply the ideas and principles I've outlined. But the longer-term solution does lie upstream. Education systems must change too to meet the radically new circumstances in which they are now operating. The economic and intellectual assumptions on which our national systems of education have been built originated in another time and for other purposes.

The challenge for education

Education must be rebalanced to conform to three principles:

- balance across the curriculum;
- balance within the teaching of disciplines; and
- balance between education and the wider world.

Frameworks and cages

In many school systems throughout the world, there is an imbalance in the curriculum. The emphasis is on science, technology, mathematics and language teaching at the expense of the arts, humanities and physical education. It is essential that there is an equal balance between these areas of the curriculum. This is necessary because each of these broad groupings of disciplines reflects major areas of cultural knowledge and experience to which all young people should have equal access. Second, each addresses a different mode of intelligence and creative development. The strengths of any individual may be in one or more of them. A narrow, unbalanced curriculum will lead to a narrow, unbalanced education for some if not all young people.

The UK system, like many systems in Europe, starts from the premise that there are ten subjects in the world and we devise a system of education to teach them. Why do educational institutions have a curriculum in the first place? There are two reasons. The first is *epistemological*; it is to do with the organisation of knowledge. A curriculum suggests that there are distinctive domains of knowledge, understanding and skills that provide a framework for teaching and learning. The categories into which we divide our experiences are very important. Beyond education, beyond institutions, people work quite comfortably without these sorts of categories. We all have categories for different purposes, but education divides the world into lumps of knowledge so that we can teach children the material, ideas, knowledge and skills that we deem to be important. There are many things that are not taught in schools. Witchcraft and necromancy are not taught in most schools. One of the functions of education is to identify the legitimate areas of cultural knowledge and experience, to put a stamp of approval on certain sorts of knowledge and experience and by implication to suggest that others are not so worthwhile. Education distinguishes between the spheres of 'orthodox and heretical culture'.[112]

When the structure of the National Curriculum in England was first announced in 1986, I went with a group of others to see the then Secretary of State for Education. We asked him what the provision would be for the arts. He told us that art and music would be the foundation subjects. 'What about dance and drama', I asked. 'Well drama, of course, is part of English', he said, 'and dance is part of physical education'. Well, of course, they are not. This is a very common mistake. Because dramatic texts are written down, they are commonly treated as literature to be read, rather than actions to be performed. Drama is an active art form not a literary one. The fact that it can be written down does not make it a textual form any more than the existence of musical notation should suggest that music is a form of Morse code. Similarly, it is a mistake to group dance with track and field events.

Physical education is primarily associated with competitive sports and with games and exercises in the gymnasium. These are extremely important. But there are important differences between athletics and dance: winning, for example. On the whole we do not come out of a performance of Swan Lake asking who won. I am a board member of the Birmingham Royal Ballet. We did not send a team to the Sydney Olympics. We are not funded by the Sports Council. These are small indications of functional differences between sport and dance. Saying that dance is part of the PE is like saying that history is really part of English because we write essays in English and in history. We use our bodies in dance and in physical education but this does not mean they are the same thing.

Dance is slotted into PE only if the starting point is that there are ten subjects in the world and everything has to be part of one of them. If so you may as well put dance with PE because it's convenient, and you're changed anyway. Outside education, these categories don't help very much. If you go to an opera performance, what is that? Is it drama? Is it music? Is it visual art? A dance performance is a physical experience for the dancers but it's a visual and musical experience for the audience. What is theatre? The best we can do is to describe these as integrated art forms. But they are not. They are only integrated in the sense that education has disintegrated them in the first place so that they can be taught.

The first function of a curriculum is epistemological. But a curriculum has a second function; this is *managerial*. Educational institutions need a curriculum so that they can organise themselves, know how many teachers to hire, what resources are needed, how to arrange the day, whom to put where, at what time and for how long. A curriculum is a management tool. What tends to happen is that the managerial functions of the curriculum eventually overtake the epistemological functions. One reason that dance is part of PE is that the UK government couldn't afford to have dance as a compulsory part of everybody's education. There weren't the teachers around to do it. If they were to commit themselves to dance as a central part of education, as they've done with science, it would have involved a massive reorganisation of teacher education and funding. But there was another reason. They saw no need to make this provision in the first place. In most education systems, the arts are not seen as sufficiently important to be at the heart of education, and it is simply taken for granted that this is the way things should be.

A distinction is commonly made between academic and non-academic subjects in schools. So pupils who are not very good at academic subjects might be encouraged to concentrate on less academic ones. Alternatively, academic subjects might be balanced in some way with non-academic subjects. Usually, for example, science or history or mathematics are seen as academic subjects and art, music or drama as non-academic. This is a basic misconception. It reinforces two assumptions, which must be rethought. The first is the very idea of subjects. This idea suggests that different areas of the curriculum are defined by their content or subject matter. Science is different from art because it deals with different subject matter.

When I first arrived at my present university, I went in the first week to a meeting of the professorial board, a committee of all professors in the university across all disciplines. There was a proposal from the professor of chemistry that the university should establish a new professorship in chemical biology. The board nodded sagely at the wisdom of this proposal and was about to move on when it was opposed by the professor of biological sciences. He argued that what the university really needed was a chair in biological chemistry. We nodded sagely again, though with a creeping sense of unease and sat back to listen to the debate. The point is that disciplines are constantly merging, reforming, cross-fertilising each other and producing new offspring. There are not ten subjects in the world but a huge variety of ways of knowing, fields of research topics and methods of inquiry. Our categories of knowledge must at best be provisional.

The second assumption is that some subjects are academic and some are not. This is not true. All issues and questions can be considered from an academic point of view and from others too. They can be investigated in the deductive mode or in other modes. Schools and universities teach many subjects but one dominant way of thinking – the verbal, mathematical, deductive and propositional. These processes can be applied to any phenomena: plants, weather, poetry, music, social systems. On this basis, the person who writes about the arts may be thought to be intellectually superior to the person who produces the work. A Picasso scholar – but not Picasso himself – may be given a PhD. Doing the arts should be recognised as being as legitimate an intellectual process as critical inquiries about the arts. The heart of this argument is that knowledge can be generated in many ways other than in words and numbers. Not all that we know can be put into words and numbers, nor is what can be put into words and numbers all that we do know.

The balance of teaching

In *Chapter Five* I distinguished between the two traditions of individualism, the *rational* and the *natural*. To some extent these have been associated with different styles of teaching. Facilitating creative development requires the teaching of knowledge and skills, together with opportunities to speculate and experiment. This is a sophisticated process that combines elements of what are thought of as traditional and progressive education. So-called traditional methods are usually associated with formal instruction to the whole class and with rote learning; progressive methods with children working individually or in groups and exploring their own interests and opinions. Real life in education is not normally as neat as this. Some teachers favour particular methods: many use a mixture. Nor is there a neat distinction in relation to my argument here. Traditional methods are associated with conventional academic standards. The apparent decline in the use of these methods is often seen as a root cause of the apparent decline in these standards.

I am not arguing against academic standards in themselves nor would I celebrate a decline in them. My concern is with the preoccupation with these standards to the exclusion of everything else. I am not arguing against formal instruction. I am not appealing for a wider use of so-called progressive teaching methods. Both have an important place in teaching. Some of these methods do put a strong emphasis on creativity: some do not. Some of this work is excellent: some is not. A common failing is the tendency to misunderstand the nature of creative activity not only in education but more generally. Too often what passes for creativity has been an undisciplined and undemanding process.

The emphasis in schools on academic learning has tended to value only one mode of knowing and, in so doing, has displaced others. This has been to the detriment of all of them. Creativity depends on interactions between feeling and thinking, and across different disciplinary boundaries and fields of ideas. New curricula must be evolved which are more permeable and which encourage a better balance between generative thinking and critical thinking in all modes of understanding.

Our systems of education are based on the view that intelligence is a linear process of rational thought. From this we have derived economic models of education which are equally linear. The reason that all countries are taking these issues so seriously now is the recognition that these old assumptions won't do any more. The economic circumstances in which we all live, and in which our children will have to make their way, are utterly different from those of 20 or even 10 years ago. For these we need different styles of education and different priorities. We are generating cultural and social circumstances within which the old processes of rationalism in themselves are increasingly inadequate. We need a new Renaissance that moves beyond these old categories and develops the relationships between different processes rather than emphasising their differences. We need to re-evaluate the relationships of areas of educational experience that are now separated. We need new structures of learning for a different type of future. We cannot meet the challenges of the 21st century with the educational ideologies of the 19th.

Education policies for the future must learn from the past but must not be dictated by it. We cannot approach the future looking backwards. We now have a school curriculum that teaches ten subjects but only limited ways of thinking. We need an education that values different modes of intelligence and sees relationships between disciplines. To achieve this, there must be a different balance of priorities between the arts, sciences and humanities in education and in the forms of thinking they promote. They should be taught in ways that reflect their intimate connections in the world beyond education. Achieving this is not easy but the benefits of success are substantial and the price of failure is high.

The ecology of human resources

I began this book by looking at the changing context of education and the rapid rate of economic and technological change. Ironically, some people resist new approaches to education precisely because they are concerned about helping people to be employable. They seem to think that arguing for more creative approaches to education and developing human resources are luxuries that are out of step with the hard-headed realities of finding work. They are not. One of Europe's leading employment agencies is Reed Executive plc. The company was founded in 1960 by Alec (now Sir Alec) Reed with an initial investment of £75, and specialised in temporary secretarial appointments. It was capitalised in 2000 at approximately £114 million and now covers an enormous range of employment opportunities in many different fields. Its development over 40 years has coincided with the profound changes in labour and employment that I have outlined here. It is now growing at a faster pace than ever and has introduced an entirely new structure and strategy to face the new realities of the world of work. The present chief executive James Reed sees the development of creative abilities as fundamental to the future success of companies and individuals alike – in all areas of employment.

'In our world that is changing so quickly and becoming so much more complex, the opportunities that are offered by new technologies and by new ways of doing business are clearly immense. We must seize these opportunities. But if we are to do so successfully, we must be creative, we must cherish the individual and we must be courageous enough to meet ever greater challenges head on. We must routinely do what has never been done before and must be obsessed with improving what we do already. In this new world the winners will be those who attract the best talent, who have the best insights and transform the way they do business to bring real and enduring value to customers.

'For certain the winners of the future will be focused and they will be fast. To this end, over the last six months we have put a new strategy and structure in place that has speed, simplicity and service at its core. At a time when our Group is larger than it has ever been, our absolute priority is to reorganise into smaller more customer focused and more commercially agile business units. We call this our Starburst strategy. At the very heart of the strategy is the belief that we will deliver much more to clients, candidates and co-members (or stars) if we create room for individual expression and for the development of distinctive client focused strategies in the different arenas in which we operate ... Our new structure with a very small central team together with the Starburst strategy means that we now look more like a venture capitalist company than a traditional business. This is deliberate, but we could choose to describe ourselves as a "Venture Peoplists". The focus of our future activities and future investment will be people first and foremost. In the new creative economy, more than ever before, it will be people and not capital that make the difference. Our philosophy has always been that been people make the difference and our future investment strategy will reflect this.'

At the heart of the new strategies that are needed for business and for education there must be a new conception of human resources. This is where the ideas about intelligence and creativity that I have developed in this book are pointing. It is fundamentally a question of ecology. The idea of ecology has had a major impact on our thinking about the natural resources of the earth. We now recognise that during the Industrial Revolution, we made very partial use of the earth's resources. We wasted or destroyed a great deal of what it had to offer because we couldn't see the value of it. Along the way we have jeopardised the balance of nature by not recognising how different elements of the environment sustain each other. Although the dangers persist, they are now understood. There is a similar calamity in our use of human resources that has not been recognised.

In the interests of the industrial economy and of academic achievement, we have subjected ourselves to a partial form of education. We have wasted or destroyed a great deal of what people had to offer because we couldn't see the value of it. Along the way we have jeopardised the balance of human nature by not recognising how different elements of our abilities sustain and enrich each other. The dangers persist, and they are not yet widely understood. Education and training are the key to the future, but a key can be turned in two directions. Turn it one way and you lock resources away, even from those they belong to. Turn it the other way and you release resources and give people back to themselves. The companies, communities and nations that succeed in future will balance their books only by solving the complex equation of human resources. Our own times are being swept along on an avalanche of innovations in science, technology, and social thought. To keep pace with these changes, or to get ahead of them, we will need all our wits about us – literally. We must learn to be creative.

ENDNOTES

1 *All Our Futures* is specifically addressed to issues in education and to the changes that are needed in schools. In *Out of Our Minds* I take a broader and a longer view of creativity in business and in education. In doing this I draw from and develop some of the conceptual arguments we present in sections of *All Our Futures*.

2 Ian Pearson, British Telecom, interviewed in *The Sunday Times*, 4 June 2000.

3 Details from *The Institute of Management*, 2 Savoy Court, Strand, London WC2R 0EZ.

4 E. Chambers *et al.*, 'The War for Talent', *McKinsey Quarterly*, 1998, No. 3.

5 Formal education for all was introduced in Britain in 1870. The government provided for all children to have a basic grounding in literacy and numeracy to the age of 12. In the closing years of World War II, the Government set about planning the post-war reconstruction of the country. Its plans for education were set out in the Education Act of 1944. One of the main aims was to provide post-elementary education for all young people.

6 Charles Ostman, *Magical Blend* magazine, No. 47, October 1998.

7 The Times, London, October 2000.

8 R. Kurzweil, 'The Coming Merging of Mind and Machine', *Scientific American*, Vol. 10, No. 3, Autumn 1999.

9 R. Kurzweil, 'The Coming Merging of Mind and Machine', *Scientific American*, Vol. 10, No. 3, Autumn 1999.

10 Fortune magazine, September 2000.

11 Department for Culture Media and Sport, *Creative Industries Mapping Exercise*, DCMS, London, 1998.

12 Information from *The Population Reference Bureau*, 1875, Connecticut Avenue, NW, Suite 520, Washington, DC 20009. www.prb.org

13 Information from *The Industrial Society*, Pall Mall, London SW1.

14 Hamish Macrae, *The World in 2010*, unpublished seminar paper.

15 New civic universities were opened in Birmingham (1900), Liverpool and Wales (1903), Leeds (1904), Sheffield (1905), Bristol (1909).

16 The Times, London, 10 May 2000.

17 Alan Smithers, Director, Centre for Education and Employment Research, Liverpool University, in *The Times*, London, 10 May 2000.

18 R. O'Connor & N. Sheehy, *Understanding Suicidal Behaviour,* British Psychological Society, London, 2000.

19 Department for Education and Employment, *Skills for All: Proposals for a National Skills Agenda*, DfEE Publications, London, 2000.

20 'Ganga': from the English word gang; a term used by police departments in the United States to describe all people of colour under 18.

21 American Creativity at Risk: Report of a National Symposium, November 1996. Details from the Geraldine R Dodge Foundation, 163 Madison Avenue, Morristown, NJ 07962, USA.

22 Mary Schmidt Campbell, Cultural Affairs Commissioner, New York, in *American Creativity at Risk: Report of a National Symposium*, November 1996.

23 Guardian, London, 27 June 2000. These figures and accounts are taking from a survey by the National Union of Teachers to members at all the city's secondary schools. Response to the survey was comparatively small – 116 useable replies – but the union is convinced they are typical. 70% of teachers who had been assaulted had more than five years' teaching experience

24 Ken Richardson, *The Making of Intelligence*, Phoenix, London, 1999.

25 These tests are taken from the official Mensa website: http://www.mensa.org.uk/. The answers are:
   Question 1: 'O'. The letters are the first and last letters of Mercury, Venus, Earth, Mars, Jupiter, Saturn, Uranus, Neptune and Pluto.
   Question 2: '140'. The alphabetical positions of all the letters are added to give the amount.
   Question 3: South 'v'. The series is: south, east, north, south, west, east spirals clockwise from the top left-hand corner.

26 Ken Richardson, *The Making of Intelligence*, Phoenix, London, 1999.

27 Ken Richardson, *The Making of Intelligence*, Phoenix, London, 1999.

28 R. Hernstein & C. Murray, *The Bell Curve: Intelligence and Class Structure in American Life*, Simon & Schuster, New York, 1996.

29 T.S. Kuhn, *The Structure of Scientific Revolutions*, Chicago University Press, Chicago, 1970.

30 S. Langer, *Philosophy in a New Key*, New American Library, New York, 1951.

31 For a fuller account of the history and roles of the grammar schools, see Robin Davis, *The Grammar School*, Penguin Books, Harmondsworth, 1967.

32 St Paul's school founded in 1518 was funded by the Mercers Company and was independent of the church. During the reign of the Tudors there was a huge increase in the foundation of grammar schools. Many schools that had been closed during Henry's dissolution of the monasteries were reopened. Schools were established by successful individuals and by the city livery companies including the Merchant Tailors. King Edward VI also promoted and lent his name to the foundation of grammar schools in many cities throughout the land. The growth of grammar schools contin-

ued under the Stewarts. One hundred and fifty-five were founded between 1501 and 1601; one hundred and eighty-six between 1601 and 1651.

33 Quoted in Robin Davis, *The Grammar School*, Penguin Books, Harmondsworth, 1967.

34 It was also seen as vital to address the manifest and to many social reformers the offensive problems of social deprivation among the labouring classes.

35 B. Simon, *Intelligence, Psychology, Education*, Lawrence Wishart, London, 1978.

36 Robin Davis, *The Grammar School*, Penguin Books, Harmondsworth, 1967.

37 This is a system known as 'norm-referencing'. It means that the assessment of individual students is based not on absolute but on relative achievement. If all candidates were to be given 'A' there would be complaints about falling standards. A pupil's placing does not depend solely on personal performance. He or she may improve performance by 100 percent over a year, but if everyone else improves similarly, personal grades will be no higher than before. To obtain a better grade a student must take it from students higher up the list by outperforming one or more of them. Moreover, children are entered in groups for examinations at the end of a course of study which they will have started at the same time: the starting and finishing point is based, for the most part, on how old they are. Two pupils do not always reach the same state of readiness for examinations at the same time even if their potential for success is the same.

38 American Creativity at Risk: Report of a National Symposium. See note 21.

39 From *Understanding Teacher Supply in Geography*, report of a conference organised by the Teacher Training Agency and the Royal Geographical Society, London, 21 April 1999. See also P. Talbot, *Careers in Geography*, Kogan Page, London, 2000.

40 Rt Hon. David Blunkett MP, Secretary of State for Education and Employment, University of Greenwich, 15 February 2000.

41 P. Scott, *The Meanings of Mass Higher Education*, Open University Press, Bristol, 1997.

42 Department of Trade and Industry, *The Future of Corporate Learning*, DTI, London, 2000.

43 Susan Greenfield, *The Human Brain: A Guided Tour*, Weidenfield & Nicholson, London, 1997.

44 C. Sagan, *The Dragons of Eden*, Coronet, London, 1978.

45 Half the problem is the way they are taught of course. The best way to learn French is to go to France and have to speak it all day with French people. The worst way is to speak it for a few minutes a week with an English person who doesn't speak it properly. This is exactly how I tried to do it. Learning a language in 30-minute periods at school is something like trying to learn to swim on dry land. It would be like balancing children on desks for 30 minutes a week miming the breast stroke and promising them that if they get the hang of it in three years' time they will be put into water. We know how they would get on.

46 R.D. Laing, *The Divided Self*, Penguin Books, Harmondsworth, 1975.

47 Howard Gardner, *Frames of Mind: The Theory of Multiple Intelligences*, Fontana, London, 1993.

48 I'm grateful to Thomas Powell, one of my graduate students, for researching this example.

49 D.A. Treffert, *Extraordinary People: Understanding 'Idiot Savants'*, Harper & Row, New York, 1989.

50 Their abilities though exceptional seem highly localised. How does this square with my argument about the interactive nature of intelligence? The point I think is that there is still a dynamic process between different capacities in the mind of the idiot savants. But in these cases it is between very high and often very low abilities in different areas of intelligence.

51 From an appreciation in *The Times*, London, February 2000.

52 He went on to become her principal partner in dance and to promote her methods in Europe in the 1970s and 1980s as principal of the London School of Contemporary Dance.

53 This can be a highly dynamic process whose eventual outcomes can be quite different from those anticipated at the outset. Sometimes the objective changes as new ideas and possibilities come into view: sometimes, as with inventions and discoveries, new purposes are found when an initial product or idea has emerged.

54 A notorious example is Carl André, the sculptor who displayed a pile of bricks in London's Tate Gallery and drew the outrage of every popular journalist.

55 See *Chapter Three*, p. 97.

56 The philosopher Edmund Husserl describes this process as *apperception*. See E. Husserl, *Logical Investigations*, Routledge and Kegan Paul, London, 1970.

57 This argument is developed by George Herbert Mead. See D.L. Miller, *George Herbert Mead: Mind, Self, Language and the World*, Texas University Press, Texas, 1973.

58 In developing this example, I am grateful for the advice and expertise of Barrie Wiggham, formerly of the Hong Kong Government and Hong Kong's Representative in Washington.

59 This is the term used by the German philosopher Alfred Schutz. See A Schutz, *The Phenomenology of the Social World*, Heinemann, London, 1972.

60 It's widely recognised, and deeply felt, for example, that our sense of time alters as we get older. In childhood, minutes can feel like hours and hours like days. Weeks, months and years seem to pass worryingly quickly the older we are.

61 James Britton, *Language and Learning*, Penguin Books, Harmondsworth, 1972.

62 M. Polanyi, , *Personal Knowledge*, Routledge and Kegan Paul, London, 1969.

63 J. Grotowski, *Towards a Poor Theatre*, Methuen, London, 1975.

64 From a filmed interview now available in the *Masters of Science* series from the Vega Trust, CPES, University of Sussex, Falmer, Brighton BN1 9QJ, UK. www.vega.org.uk. The Vega Trust was established to promote and deepen public understanding of the processes and excitement of science. One of its leading figures is the distinguished chemist and Nobel laureate, Professor Sir Harry Kroto.

65 S. Langer, *Philosophy in a New Key*, New American Library, New York, 1951.

66 George Kelly, *A Theory of Personality: The Psychology of Personal Constructs*, W W Norton & Co., New York, 1963.

67 I'm grateful to John Haycraft, the distinguished English auctioneer and valuer for helpful background information and advice.

68 See note 64.

69 A. Koestler, *The Act of Creation*, Picador, London, 1975.

70 D. Goleman, *Emotional Intelligence*, Bloomsbury, London, 1996. A report in 1999 by the Mental Health Foundation, *The Big Picture*, gives graphic evidence of this among children at school.

71 Quoted by Peter Abbs in 'Education and the Expressive Disciplines', *Tract*, No. 25, The Gryphon Press.

72 S. Langer, *Philosophy in a New Key*, New American Library, New York, 1951.

73 J.W. Carey, *The Antioch Review*, XXXVII, Yellow Springs, Ohio, 1967

74 James Hemmings, *The Betrayal of Youth*, Marion Boyars, London, 1980.

75 In the early 1970s, Robert Witkin, a British sociologist, published a book looking at the creative processes of the arts. He called it *The Intelligence of Feeling*. He develops in a different way some of the themes that are elaborated in detail in Daniel Goleman's book published in 1996 entitled *Emotional Intelligence* (see note 77 below).

76 In certain cases, of course, emotional states are caused by physical disturbances as in some forms of depression or through the metabolic changes associated with illness.

77 D. Goleman, *Emotional Intelligence*, Bloomsbury, London, 1996.

78 D. Goleman, *Emotional Intelligence*, Bloomsbury, London, 1996.

79 D. Goleman, *Emotional Intelligence*, Bloomsbury, London, 1996.

80 Karl Popper, *Conjectures and Refutations: The Growth of Scientific Knowledge*, Routledge and Kegan Paul, London, 1969.

81 Brian Simon, *Intelligence, Psychology, Education*, Lawrence Wishart, London, 1978.

82 M. Polanyi, *Personal Knowledge*, Routledge and Kegan Paul, London, 1969.

83 E. Pivcevic, *Husserl and Phenomenology*, Hutchinson University Library, 1970.

84 R. Descartes, *A Discourse on Method*, transl. F.E. Sutcliffe, Penguin Books, Harmondsworth, 1968.

85 E.M. Forster, *Two Cheers for Democracy*, Penguin Books, Harmondswoth, 1974.

86 Board of Education, *Report on Primary Schools*, HMSO, London, 1932.

87 It is commonly said that the literal meaning of education is to draw out, from the Latin word *educo*. The more common Latin word for drawing out is *educere*, a third conjugation verb, which gives us the English words 'educe' and 'eduction'. But education derives from *educare*, a first conjugation verb meaning to bring up or educate. So this doesn't really help.

88 Sir Herbert Read in Joint Council for Education Through Art, *A Consideration of Humanity, Technology and Education in Our Time*, Report of the Conference at the Royal Festival Hall, London, 22–27 April 1957.

89 R.W. Siroka *et al.* (eds), *Sensitivity Training and Group Encounter*, Grosset and Dunlop, 1971.

90 V. Frankl, *Psychotherapy and Existentialism*, Souvenir Press, London, 1970.

91 L.A. Reid, *Yesterday's Today: A Journey into Philosophy*, unpublished autobiography, 1980.

92 Ministries of culture throughout the world and national cultural policies often focus particularly on the arts.

93 James Britton, *Language and Learning*, Penguin Books, Harmondsworth, 1972.

94 D. Lawton, *Class, Culture and Curriculum*, Routledge and Kegan Paul, London, 1975.

95 Raymond Williams, *The Long Revolution*, Penguin Books, Harmondsworth, 1966.

96 M. Polanyi, *Personal Knowledge*, Routledge and Kegan Paul, London, 1969.

97 This idea was developed by the cultural theorist Walter Benjamin in a celebrated essay, 'The Work of Art in the Age of Mechanical Reproduction', in W. Benjamin, *Illuminations*, Fontana, London, 1980.

98 Just as painters feared that photography would be the death of painting, theatres feared that film would be the death of their art form. Neither of these proved to be true. In the medium term, theatre was released into a new period of great invention and innovation, from the 1920s to the 1950s in particular.

99 Clifford Geertz, *The Interpretation of Cultures*, Chicago University Press, Chicago, 1975.

100 Department for Education and Employment, *All Our Futures: Creativity, Culture and Education*, HMSO, London, 1999. For a fascinating discussion of the growing links between the arts and sciences, see S. Ede, *Strange and Charmed*, Calouste Gulbenkian Foundation, London, 2000.

101 N. Frye, *The Stubborn Structure: Essays on Criticism and Society*, Methuen, London, 1970.

102 The idea of modernism fired intellectual energies to the late 1960s. They were gradually replaced by new ways of thinking that have come to be grouped under a general heading of postmodernism.

103 M. Levitas, *Marxist Perspectives in the Sociology of Education*, Routledge and Kegan Paul, London, 1974.

104 The emergence of modernism in painting in Europe marked a break with the formal structures and constraints of the classical tradition. The great

movements in Western Europe in painting are characterised by painters turning to new frameworks of creative expression. The Impressionists aimed to break free from the existing preoccupations with figurative painting. They wanted to explore the use of colour and texture as a way of capturing the feelings they experienced in contemplating their subjects rather than in trying accurately to reproduce their physical appearances.

105 T. Peters & R.H. Waterman, *In Search of Excellence*, Harper & Row, New York, 1982.

106 For a comprehensive survey of the development of creativity testing see R.J. Sternberg, *The Handbook of Creativity*, Cambridge University Press, Cambridge, 1999.

107 For a useful summary of these and other techniques, see Ros Jay, *The Ultimate Book of Business Creativity*, Capstone Publishing, Oxford, 2000.

108 E. Chambers, E *et al.*, 'The War for Talent', *McKinsey Quarterly*, No. 3, pp 44–57, 1998.

109 Quoted in *American Creativity in Crisis*: report of a national symposium.

110 Quoted in *American Creativity in Crisis*: report of a national symposium.

111 From an article by John Carvel in the *Guardian*, London, 2 October 2000.

112 P. Bourdieu, 'Systems of Education and Systems of Thought', in M.F.D. Young (ed.), *Knowledge and Control*, Collier MacMillan, London, 1971.

REFERENCES

Abbs, P., 'Education and the Expressive Disciplines', *Tract*, No. 25, The Gryphon Press.

Bajer, J., 'The Paradox of the Talents' in *People Management Magazine*, December 1999

Benjamin, W., *Illuminations*, Fontana, London, 1980.

Board of Education, *Report on Primary Schools*, HMSO, London, 1932.

Boden, M., *The Creative Mind*, Abacus, London, 1994.

Bourdieu, P., 'Systems of Education and Systems of Thought', in M.F.D. Young (ed.) *Knowledge and Control*, Collier MacMillan, 1971.

Britton, J., *Language and Learning*, Penguin Books, Harmondsworth, 1972.

Britton, J. *et al.*, *The Development of Writing Abilities: 11–18*, Macmillan Education, London, 1975.

Carey, J.W., *The Antioch Review*, XXXVII, Yellow Springs, Ohio, 1967.

Chambers, E. *et al.*, 'The War for Talent', *McKinsey Quarterly*, No. 3, pp 44–57, 1998.

Davis, R., *The Grammar School*, Penguin Books, Harmondsworth, 1967.

Department for Culture, Media and Sport, *Creative Industries Mapping Exercise*, DCMS, London, 1998.

Department for Education and Employment, *All Our Futures: Creativity, Culture and Education*, HMSO, London, 1999.

Department for Education and Employment, *Skills for All: Proposals for a National Skills Agenda*, DfEE Publications, London, 2000.

Department for Trade and Industry, *The Future of Corporate Learning*, HMSO, London, 2000.

Descartes, R., *A Discourse on Method*, transl. Sutcliffe, F.E., Penguin Books, Harmondsworth, 1968.

Ede, S., *Strange and Charmed*, Calouste Gulbenkian Foundation, London, 2000.

Forster, E.M., *Two Cheers for Democracy*, Penguin Books, Harmondswoth, 1974.

Frankl, V., *Psychotherapy and Existentialism*, Souvenir Press, London, 1970.

Gardner, H., *Frames of Mind: The Theory of Multiple Intelligences*, Fontana, London, 1993.

Geertz, C., *The Interpretation of Cultures*, Chicago University Press, Chicago, 1975.

Goleman, G., *Emotional Intelligence*, Bloomsbury, London, 1996.

Gould, S.J., *The Mismeasure of Man*, W W Norton & Co., New York, 1996.

Greenfield, S., *The Human Brain: A Guided Tour*, Weidenfield & Nicholson, London, 1997.

Grotowski, J., *Towards a Poor Theatre*, Methuen, London, 1975.

Hemmings, J., *The Betrayal of Youth*, Marion Boyars, London, 1980.

Hernstein, R. & Murray, C., *The Bell Curve: Intelligence and Class Structure in American Life*, Simon & Schuster, New York, 1996.

Husserl, E., *Logical Investigations*, Routledge and Kegan Paul, London, 1970.

Jay, R., *The Ultimate Book of Business Creativity*, Capstone Publishing, Oxford, 2000.

Joint Council for Education Through Art, *A Consideration of Humanity, Technology and Education in Our Time*, Report of the Conference at the Royal Festival Hall, London, 22–27 April 1957.

Jung, C.G., *Modern Man in Search of a Soul*, Routledge and Kegan Paul, London, 1933.

Kelly, G.A., *A Theory of Personality: The Psychology of Personal Constructs*, W W Norton & Co., New York, 1963.

Koestler, A., *The Act of Creation*, Picador, London, 1975.

Kuhn, T.S., *The Structure of Scientific Revolutions*, Chicago University Press, Chicago, 1970.

Kurzweil, R., 'The Coming Merging of Mind and Machine', *Scientific American*, Vol. 10, No. 3, Autumn 1999.

Langer, S., *Philosophy in a New Key*, New American Library, New York, 1951.

Laing, R.D., *The Divided Self*, Penguin Books, Harmondsworth, 1975.

Lawton, D., *Class, Culture and Curriculum*, Routledge and Kegan Paul, London, 1975.

Levitas, M., *Marxist Perspectives in the Sociology of Education*, Routledge and Kegan Paul, London, 1974.

Mental Health Foundation, *The Big Picture*, The Mental Health Foundation, London, 1999.

Miller, A.I., *Insights of Genius: Imagery and Creativity in Art and Science*, Springer-Verlag, New York, 1996.

Miller, D.L., *George Herbert Mead: Mind, Self, Language and the World*, Texas University Press, 1973.

O'Connor, R., Sheehy, N., *Understanding Suicidal Behaviour*, British Psychological Society, London, 2000.

O'Donohue, J., *Anam Cara*, Bantam, London, 1998.

Ostman, C., 'Techno Marvels in the Making', *Magical Blend* magazine, No. 47, October 1998.

Peters, T., Waterman, R.H., *In Search of Excellence*, Harper & Row, New York, 1982.

Pivcevic, E., *Husserl and Phenomenology*, Hutchinson University Library, 1970.

Polanyi, M., *Personal Knowledge*, Routledge and Kegan Paul, London, 1969.

Popper, K., *Conjectures and Refutations: The Growth of Scientific Knowledge*, Routledge and Kegan Paul, London, 1969.

Rada, J.F., *The Metamorphosis of the Word: Libraries With a Future*, Fifth Mortenson Memorial Lecture, University of Illinois, Urbana Champaign, 7 October 1994. Unpublished.

Reid, L.A., *Yesterday's Today: A Journey into Philosophy*, unpublished autobiography, 1980.

Richardson, K., *The Making of Intelligence*, Phoenix, London, 1999.

Rogers, C., *Freedom to Learn*, Merrill, New York, 1969.

Russell, B., *The Problems of Philosophy*, Oxford University Press, Oxford, 1970.

Sagan, C., *The Dragons of Eden*, Coronet, London, 1978.

Schutz, A., *The Phenomenology of the Social World*, Heinemann, London, 1972.

Scott, P., *The Meanings of Mass Higher Education*, Open University Press, Bristol, 1997.

Simon, B., *Intelligence, Psychology, Education*, Lawrence Wishart, London, 1978.

Siroka, R.W. *et al.* (eds), *Sensitivity Training and Group Encounter*, Grosset & Dunlop, 1971.

Sternberg, R.J., *The Handbook of Creativity*, Cambridge University Press, Cambridge, 1999.

Talbot, P., *Careers in Geography*, Kogan Page, London, 2000.

Toffler, A., *Future Shock*, Random House, New York, 1970.

Treffert, D.A. *Extraordinary People: Understanding 'Idiot Savants'*, Harper & Row, New York, 1989.

Williams, R., *The Long Revolution*, Penguin Books, Harmondsworth, 1966.

Witkin, R., *The Intelligence of Feeling*, Heinemann, London, 1974.

Yeats, W.B., Collected Poems, Macmillan, London, 1978.

INDEX

ABOUT THE AUTHOR

Sir Ken Robinson is an internationally recognized leader in the development of creativity, innovation and human resources. He has worked with governments in Europe, Asia and the USA, with international agencies, Fortune 500 companies, not-for-profit corporations and some of the world's leading cultural organizations. They include the Royal Shakespeare Company, Sir Paul McCartney's Liverpool Institute for Performing Arts, the Royal Ballet, the Hong Academy for Performing Arts, the European Commission, UNESCO, the Council of Europe, the J Paul Getty Trust and the Education Commission of the States.

In 1998, he led a national commission on creativity, education and the economy for the UK Government, bringing together leading business people, scientists, artists and educators. The resulting report, <u>All Our Futures: Creativity Culture and Education</u> (The Robinson Report) was published to wide acclaim. The London Times said, *'This report should have every chief executive officer and human resources director in the country thumping the table and demanding action. It raises some of the most serious and far-reaching issues affecting business and education in the next century.'*

He was the central figure in developing a strategy for creative and economic development as part of the Peace Process in Northern Ireland, working with the ministers for training, education enterprise and culture. The resulting blueprint for change, <u>Unlocking Creativity</u>, was adopted by politicians of all parties and by business, education and cultural leaders across the Province. He was one of four international advisors to the Singapore Government for its strategy to become the creative hub of South East Asia.

For ten years he was Professor of Education at the University of Warwick in England and is now Professor Emeritus. He is in wide demand as an inspirational speaker with a unique talent for conveying profoundly serious messages with enormous humour and passion and wit. He speaks to audiences throughout the world on the changing needs of business, education and organizations in the new global economies. In 2001, he was voted SfB Business Speaker of the Year by over 200 global and European companies. In 2005, he was named one of Time/Fortune/CNN's 'Principal Voices'. In 2003, he was knighted by Queen Elizabeth II for services to the arts.

'Thank you so much for making our closing address one of our most outstanding presentations ever! I can't say enough about your fantastic content and your humorous style and the range and depth of your portfolio topics. Thank you for a first class address. We couldn't have asked for anyone better!'

Richmond Events, New York NY

'The event was a wonderful success with you as the primary reason. Many people told me later that you were the best YPO speaker they have ever heard. I respectfully disagree, because I think you are the best speaker I have heard period.'

CEO & President, SMN Healthcare Inc.

'On behalf of the International Music Products Association, I am writing to express our appreciation for your presentation at the Fifth Global Economic. Your passion is apparent, and your preparation and research were exemplary, establishing your presentation as a perfect complement to the Summit agenda.'

National Association of Music Merchants

'You were fantastic! Your insights into creativity in business are "spot on" for what we do. It will be remembered as one of the great WEO events.'

World Entrepreneurs Organization, St. Louis

'As usual you captured the audience with you great humor and brilliant delivery. You were a major contributor in making this event such a huge success.'

British American Business Council, Manufacturing Conference, Long Beach, CA.

'The feedback has been overwhelmingly positive. The best speaker we have ever had.'

The World Bank, Global Human Resources Conference, Washington

'Your talk at the KPMG event was quite the most remarkable piece of public speaking I have ever been privileged to witness. Not only did you have me in stitches practically the whole way through, your line of argument was coherent and extremely powerful.'

3SIXTY Company, UK

'He has that rare gift of being able to draw people along on a current of laughter and then pull them up short with powerful messages about the human condition.'

Ministry of Defense, UK

'You were a magnificent keynote speaker. As I'm sure you could tell from the response in the hall, your words resonated deeply with your audience. Your combination of insight, anecdote, historical perspective, and humor was absolutely perfect for the occasion. I'm continually getting calls about the conference and universally you are mentioned as the highlight.'

Arts in Education Roundtable, New York City

'He left the whole of York buzzing with excitement and recalling things he had said (it's a bit like Python fans recalling the dead parrot sketch). Sir Ken's lecture was quite brilliant and he has done a huge amount to lift morale and make everybody feel enthused again about education whether they are teachers, head teachers or advisers.'

City of York Annual Lecture, UK

'Orange County is a buzz about you. You were spectacular. Thank you so much for presenting at our February meeting. You were truly the most outstanding guest we have had in many years. Your message was delivered with humor and the utmost class.'

California Association of School Administrators, Anaheim

'Ken Robinson is way funnier than I'll ever be. If I'd had him when I was at UCLA, I wouldn't have skipped so many classes.'

Rob Reiner, actor

Contact Ken Robinson at:

www.sfb.co.uk
www.sirkenrobinson.com